THE ART OF ALLUSION IN VICTORIAN FICTION

THE ART OF ALLUSION IN VICTORIAN FICTION

Michael Wheeler

First published 1979 by
THE MACMILLAN PRESS LTD
London and Basingstoke
Associated companies in Delhi
Dublin Hong Kong Johannesburg Lagos
Melbourne New York Singapore Tokyo

Photoset in Great Britain by
Vantage Photosetting Co., Ltd,
Southampton

Printed by Unwin Brothers Ltd.
The Gresham Press,
Old Woking, Surrey

British Library Cataloguing in Publication Data

Wheeler, Michael
 The art of allusion in Victorian fiction
 1. Allusions   2. English fiction – 19th century –
History and criticism
 I. Title
 823'.8'09   PR830.A/

 ISBN 0–333–24010–3

For Viv

Contents

Preface

My aim in this book is to argue that the use of literary and biblical allusion should be recognised as an important convention in Victorian fiction, and that the modern reader can understand the fiction more fully if he understands the convention. The first two chapters are introductory, examining the aesthetics of allusion, Victorian habits of quotation and reference in various contexts, such as religious worship, and the functions of allusion in the fiction. The next seven chapters are new readings of famous novels which have been chosen to illustrate what I consider to be the most important and interesting ways in which allusion is used in the period. These novels vary in type, and their dates of publication range from the 1840s to the 1890s. Yet each highly individual writer works within the same convention of allusion, developing themes and images, plot motifs and the portrayal of character around clusters of quotations and references. Whereas the earlier novelists quoted or referred to works which were familiar to a wide range of readers, thus helping them to understand the fiction, later novelists used allusions more self-consciously and less directly. In the last chapter I touch on certain developments in early twentieth-century fiction before making some general concluding remarks on the art of allusion in Victorian fiction. In tackling a subject as large and comparatively unexplored as this my initial problem was one of selection, and I hope that the reader will go on to consider other texts by other novelists, applying and perhaps modifying the principles I attempt to define.

The following editions of the selected novels are quoted:

Charlotte Brontë, *Jane Eyre*, edited by Jane Jack and Margaret Smith, Clarendon Edition (Oxford, 1969).

Elizabeth Gaskell, *Mary Barton and Other Tales*, vol. I of *The Works of Mrs. Gaskell*, edited by A. W. Ward, 8 vols (London, 1906).

Charles Dickens, *Hard Times*, edited by George Ford and Sylvère Monod, Norton Critical Edition (New York, 1966).

George Eliot, *Middlemarch*, edited by Gordon S. Haight, Riverside Edition (Boston, 1956).

George Meredith, *The Egoist*, vols XV and XVI (1897) of the *Works of George Meredith* [De Luxe Edition] 39 vols (London, 1896–1912).

Mary [Mrs Humphry] Ward, *Robert Elsmere*, edited by Clyde de L. Ryals, Bison Edition (Lincoln, USA, 1967).

Thomas Hardy, *Tess of the d'Urbervilles* and *The Return of the Native*, vols I and IV (1912) of *The Works of Thomas Hardy in Prose and Verse*, Wessex Edition, 24 vols (London, 1912–31).

References to these novels are by chapter or by book and chapter, in roman and arabic numerals respectively, immediately after quotations in the text. Obvious and unimportant misprints have been silently corrected. Initial letters are capitalised and final full stops inserted in inset quotations, irrespective of the case and punctuation used in the original. Italicised words in quotations are thus in the original, unless otherwise stated. In order to keep annotation to a minimum, further references to works cited at the end of the book are given in abbreviated form after quotations in the text.

Passages from chapters 1, 3 and 4 have appeared in *The British Journal of Aesthetics*, 17 (1977), and *Brontë Society Transactions*, 17 (1976). They are reprinted here by kind permission of the editors. I am grateful to the British Library for permission to quote from the manuscripts of *Middlemarch* and *Tess of the d'Urbervilles*, and from the Gladstone Papers, and to the library of University College, Dublin, for permission to quote from the manuscript of *The Return of the Native*. I would also like to thank friends at Lancaster who have helped me in various ways, including Susan Auty, Tess Cosslett, Anne Dalton, Joy Turvey and Christopher Walsh, and especially David Carroll and Richard Dutton, whose advice has been invaluable.

August 1978   MDW

1

Allusion

Every reader of literature must have noticed that writers often quote the works of others. In most readers' minds, however, quotations and references, the two basic types of allusion, are usually lumped together with such things as book illustrations, chapter titles, and 'arguments' which head chapters or cantos, all of which are ignored too easily, or dismissed as virtually redundant elements of a literary text. Some critics who have written on allusion have helped to perpetuate misconceptions which tend to place the subject in the curio category. For example, E. E. Kellett wrote as if spotting the allusions in literature were a game designed for the educated gentleman, as quoting the Classics was in the Houses of Parliament at one time. For him the best allusions are the 'natural overflow of a rich and well-stored mind', and the best reader can respond to 'veiled quotations' which give him a *slight* titillation of the memory'.[1] Although classical scholars have long recognised that allusion is a crucial indicator of the relationship between a given work and a literary tradition, the aspects of allusion on which students of English literature focused attention in the past tended to be merely curious or titillating. However, serious interest in the functions of allusion in a literary text, and the theoretical issues which those functions raise, has begun to develop in recent years. Herman Meyer's study, *The Poetics of Quotation in the European Novel* (1968), translated from the original German version of 1961, remains the most valuable critical discussion of allusion in fiction. After an excellent introductory discussion of the 'poetics of quotation', he sets about inquiring 'what the literary quotation signifies and achieves as a structural element in the novel from Rabelais to the present',[2] examining the 'Great Humorists' (Rabelais, Cervantes and Sterne) and the 'Art

1

of Quoting in Germany' from Wieland to Mann. Of the numerous critics who have discussed allusion in poetry, particularly in
relation to poetic tradition, Harold Bloom stands out as the most
challenging and provocative. In his books on literary influence
and poetic tradition, Bloom discusses allusion as one means of
Freudian defence by which poets have tried to maintain their
literary identities in the shadow of their precursors. For example,
he states that Milton's 'handling of allusion is his highly individual and original defense against poetic tradition, his revisio-
nary stance in writing what is in effect a tertiary epic'.[3] Ziva
Ben-Porat, another modern scholar who has examined the 'Poetics of Literary Allusion', defines literary allusion as 'a device for
the simultaneous activation of two texts', and, adopting Jakob-
son's terms, distinguishes between 'metaphoric' and
'metonymic' allusions. Ben-Porat's article is an important contribution to literary theory, offering a detailed analysis of the
ways in which the 'alluding text' and the 'evoked text' are
'activated'.[4]

Whereas both Bloom and Ben-Porat have a penchant for
elaborate critical terminology, Meyer tends to use rather broad
terms when discussing allusion. In the absence of received
critical terms I must suggest certain definitions before proceed-
ing further. One of the problems involved in attempting such
definitions is posed by the universality of quotation-source
relationships between individual examples of categories or
types. Emerson wrote: 'Every book is a quotation; and every
house is a quotation out of all forests, and mines, and stone
quarries; and every man is a quotation from all ancestors.'[5] As
we turn to specifically literary matters we must bear this statement in mind, for it is often extremely difficult to trace the
boundaries between generic affinities, such as vague stylistic
similarities in a large number of Victorian tracts, and specific
allusions to literary texts. Suffice it to say for the moment,
however, that my subject is strictly literary, and that the following definitions all apply to novelists' allusions which establish
some kind of relationship with earlier or contemporary literary
works. An *adopted text* is a work or part of a work from which
material is borrowed in the act of quoting or referring, and an
adoptive text is a work in which that material is placed. A
quotation is an identifiable word, phrase or passage taken from
an adopted text. A *marked quotation* is one whose nature is

indicated by means of punctuation or typography, whereas an *unmarked quotation* is one whose nature is not thus indicated. A *reference* is a word, phrase or passage which directs attention to an adopted text but which does not share stylistic similarities with it. *Allusion* is the generic term for quotations and references, and for the act of quoting or referring.

Following the *OED*, Harold Bloom has suggested that the meaning of *allusion* which I adopt is 'incorrect':

The history of 'allusion' as an English word goes from an initial meaning of 'illusion' on to an early Renaissance use as meaning a pun, or word-play in general. But by the time of Bacon it meant any symbolic likening, whether in allegory, parable or metaphor, as when in *The Advancement of Learning* poetry is divided into 'narrative, representative, and allusive.' A fourth meaning, which is still the correct modern one, follows rapidly by the very early seventeenth century, and involves any implied, indirect or hidden reference. The fifth meaning, still incorrect but bound to establish itself, now equates allusion with direct, overt reference. Since the root meaning is 'to play with, mock, jest at,' allusion is uneasily allied to words like 'ludicrous' and 'elusion'.

(Bloom, *A Map*, p. 126)

The fifth meaning is establishing itself already, often being applied to *marked quotations, unmarked quotations,* and *references.*[6] I use *allusion* in this generic sense for two reasons: first, it is now part of critical usage, and secondly, no other word, such as *quotation* or *reference*, will do. Bloom's fourth (*OED*) meaning certainly confuses the issue, as modern critics often use *allusion* in this sense. Bloom does not, however, make the important distinction between what I call an *unmarked quotation* and a *reference*. Both can be *allusions* in his fourth sense, but each has qualities which clearly differentiate it from the other. *Quotation* will not do as the generic term, as *references* are specifically not *quotations*, whereas *allusion* in my generic sense can comfortably accommodate *quotations* and *references*. The old meanings of *allusion* (word-play or symbolic likening) are not finally eradicated as soon as its fourth (modern) meaning gives way to the fifth, as Bloom seems to suggest. The 'play' between adopted and adoptive texts generated by a *marked quotation* can be as verbally witty or symbolically imaginative as an 'implied, indirect or hidden reference'. Furthermore, Bloom's anxiety concerning the uneasy alliance between *allusion* and words like 'ludicrous' and 'elusion' can be eased by pointing to the parodic nature of a large proportion of literary *allusions* down the centuries.

A brief examination of a famous passage of prose will help to clarify what I mean by the terms listed above and to illustrate some of the ways in which a reader can locate and respond to allusions:

> Now since these dead bones have already out-lasted the living ones of *Methuselah*, and in a yard under ground, and thin walls of clay, out-worn all the strong and specious buildings above it; and quietly rested under the drums and tramplings of three conquests; what Prince can promise such diuturnity unto his Reliques, or might not gladly say,
> *Sic ego componi versus in ossa velim.*[a]
> Time which antiquates Antiquities, and hath an art to make dust of all things, hath yet spared these *minor* Monuments.
> [a] Tibullus
>
> Thomas Browne, *Hydriotaphia, Urn-burial* (5)

It would be difficult to miss the two allusions in this passage which are italicised and thus eye-catching: the reference to Methuselah, who died aged 969 (Genesis 5.27), and the inset marked quotation from Tibullus's *Elegies* (III.2.26), ascribed to the author by Browne in one of his many 'marginal illustrations' in the text. Most modern readers probably know who Methuselah was, even if their knowledge of the Bible is scanty. But how many could translate the Latin or, far less likely, place the line in its context in the adopted text – the *Elegies*? In the twentieth century, editors of *Urn-burial* have thought it necessary to translate and cite exact locations for classical quotations. It is certainly important to know what the Tibullus quotation means: 'Thus should I wish to be laid to rest when turned to bones.' In a passage in which 'bones', 'clay' and 'dust' are discussed, the word *ossa* (bones) should alert the reader to the possibility that the marked quotation may be more than merely an apt statement borrowed from a classical and therefore venerable work. The presence of the marked quotation may indicate that Tibullus's *Elegies* is the adopted text for some other (un-marked) quotations in the Browne passage. But first, what is the reader to make of the English words, 'bones', 'clay' and 'dust'? Are they more than commonplace words with non-literary con-notations? Let us take them in order.

I did not recall an example of the collocation 'dead bones' in a work published before *Urn-burial* (1658) until I consulted a dictionary of quotations and found this line from Clarence's description of his shipwreck nightmare in *Richard III*: 'And mock'd the dead bones that lay scatt'red by' (I.4.33). Browne's 'dead bones' could be read as a quotation from the speech only if other stylistic similarities between the adopted and adoptive texts, or obvious contextual parallels, supported such a reading. The context in the play is altogether too watery for Browne's dusty subject. I associate 'dead bones' with two biblical pas-sages: the terrifying description of the valley which was full of 'dry bones' into which God breathed life (Ezekiel 37), and the contextually appropriate verse from Christ's attack on the scribes and Pharisees: 'ye are like unto whited sepulchres, which indeed appear beautiful outward, but are within full of dead men's bones, and of all uncleanness' (Matthew 23.27).Whether Browne *intended* me to associate his urns with whited sepulchres must remain a moot point, as 'dead bones' is not the same as 'dead men's bones', and without at least one more specific allusion to the same verse in the vicinity of 'dead bones' in Browne's text it is impossible to tell. (The opening of chapter 3 – 'Playstered and whited Sepulchres were anciently affected' – is perhaps too far removed from the opening of chapter 5 to signify.) I have to assume that 'dead bones' is not an unmarked quotation.

Like 'bones' and 'dust', 'clay' was commonly associated with death and the frailty of mortal flesh by seventeenth-century writers. The first and most obvious meaning of Browne's 'thin walls of clay' is clarified by the contrast with the 'strong and specious buildings' above ground: he is talking about the urn's 'walls'. The second meaning is generated by Browne's skilful use of a familiar conceit: the human body (or here, the 'bones') as the house, made of clay, in which the spirit resides. The body is described as 'clay' and 'dust' in the Book of Job, where the words are generally juxtaposed: 'How much less in them that dwell in houses of clay, whose foundation is in the dust, which are crushed before the moth' (Job 4.19; cf.10.9, 13.12, 27.16). The proximity of 'clay' and 'dust' in the Browne passage, reminiscent of Job, makes the buildings-walls-body associations more complex, suggesting a third meaning for 'clay': the yard of earth above the urn. Add to this the meaning of 'dust' in the famous passage from the order of the Burial of the Dead in the Book of Common Prayer ('ashes to ashes, dust to dust') and it becomes obvious that the bones-clay-dust cluster cannot be separated easily, either in terms of simple meaning or of biblical associations. The problem of locating specific adopted texts becomes doubly complicated when one returns to Tibullus's *Elegies* and finds a description of bones and ashes burnt on a funeral pyre in a passage which is admittedly distant from the line quoted by Browne (I.3.5–8). The variety of Browne's allusions reflects the scholarly syncretism of *Urn-burial*. The power of his writing, however, often depends upon the resonance of commonplace words, such as 'bones', 'clay' and 'dust', rather than associations suggested by specific quotations or references. The Methuselah reference and the marked quotation from Tibullus have quite different effects from those of words or phrases which have come down to us through a whole series of sources, literary and non-literary, until no one source can be isolated as an adopted text.

In order to decide whether a word, phrase or passage is an unmarked quotation, the reader can apply various tests to the putative adopted and adoptive texts. The former must obviously antedate the latter, and the later writer must have had access to the adopted text. If the reader notices that the style of a passage in the adoptive text seems markedly different from that of the paragraph in which it is embedded, he might hunt through author concordances, Cruden's biblical concordance and dictionaries of quotations, and discover that the passage is an unmarked quotation. Indeed, if the standard works of literature were all on tape, and if limitless computer time were available, he could make use of computers to locate numerous examples of particular collocations in the way that the dictionary of quotations supplied me with one earlier example of 'dead bones' in Shakespeare. Even if the publishers of concordances were to pool their computer tapes and a tape library of world literature were built up, however, only the mechanical business of locating a passage in an unfamiliar adopted text would have been facilitated.[7] The reader's response to an allusion which he recognises as he reads, and whose context in its adopted text is familiar to him, is obviously more spontaneous, and generally stronger and more rewarding, than his response to an allusion located with the help of reference books or computers can ever be.

When Herman Meyer is differentiating between the use of sources and the technique of allusion, he rightly mentions the pleasure which the reader can have in responding to allusion. He states that the 'borrowing is distinguished from the quotation by the fact that it has no referential character', and that the 'discovery' of a borrowing results in 'no aesthetic delight' (Meyer, pp. 7–8). As the distinctions between what Meyer calls 'borrowings' and 'quotations' are relevant to much of what follows, they should be examined more closely.

Although the differences between the relationships which we usually call influence and the relationships indicated by allusion are often difficult to recognise and explain, one can say that the critic who discusses sources and literary influence is concerned mainly with hidden pressures on authors which are often unnoticed by the reader, whereas the critic who examines allusion is mapping areas which are open to inquiry and indeed often explicitly invite examination. The critic who tends to shy away from speculation on biographical sources, literary sources and literary influence can usually examine allusion (often an indicator of inter-textual rather than inter-authorial relations) with an easy conscience. In Wimsatt's and Beardsley's famous essay on the 'Intentional Fallacy' (1946), Lowes's *Road to Xanadu*, a *locus classicus* for the source-hunter and a familiar butt of the 'clean text' man, is subjected to searching analysis, behind which lies the uneasiness which most readers of the book must have felt: that here is a critic trying to explore the necessarily secret workings of the imagination and often using external evidence in order to support his theories when the internal evidence of the poetry itself does not supply him with enough data to work on.[8] Wimsatt develops an important point which is related to his early criticism of Lowes in a more recent (1968) essay on intention: 'The search for the author's generative intention as context of the poem is a search for a temporal moment which must, as the author and the poem live on, recede and ever recede into the forgotten, as all moments do.'[9] *The Road to Xanadu* is an extreme example of an attempted reconstruction of the 'author's generative intention as context of the poem' through a 'search for a temporal moment': in this case, the moments of Coleridge's reading and writing. A reader of past literature usually has to hold in tension the antiquarian instinct to reconstruct the context in which a work was written and the historical instinct to view it in hindsight from his own time and place. Lowes bends all his critical faculties to the reconstruction of the elusive past. But he uses Wimsatt's and Beardsley's 'external' and 'intermediate' evidence: 'revelations' about 'how or why the poet wrote the poem' and 'evidence about the character of the author or about private or semiprivate meanings attached to words or topics by an author or by a coterie of which he is a member'.[10] I believe that a critic recognising allusions in a historical text has to make some kind of reconstructive move towards understanding the 'temporal moment' of publication (rather than writing). Whereas the critic who analyses literary influence, however, is likely to stray from internal evidence (the 'semantics and syntax' of a work) to external evidence, first showing how a similarity between two texts suggests influence and then that the writer of the adoptive text admits in his letters that he read the adopted text, the critic who analyses allusion can usually concentrate wholly on adopted and adoptive texts, and use only internal and intermediate evidence, valid even for the anti-intentionalist. It is to the 'temporal moments' of the publication of Victorian novels, and to the functions of allusion in the fiction, that I now turn.

2

Victorian Novels and Readers

I

The early chapters of George Meredith's *Adventures of Harry Richmond* (1871) are strange and disturbing. As Harry is whisked from place to place it is sometimes difficult to judge whether the character or his creator is losing control and direction. The reader is provided with signposts along the route, however, pointers to the kind of journey on which the hero is bound. When he and Temple are lost in a London pea-souper he climbs a lamp-post in order to consult his watch. On descending, he sees that a man is questioning Temple, with his hands on his shoulders. The man groans, saying, 'My son! I've lost my son', and walks away, leaving Harry 'overcome' (11). This is a moment of real and metaphorical illumination for Harry, when he sees that his search for his own father in London gives him a purpose in life.

Like so many memorable episodes in Victorian fiction, this incident depends for its effect upon the use of the location (the fog-bound street with its lamp-post) in which the character is placed. What follows is also characteristic of the genre, but appeals to the imagination in a quite different way. Having 'talked of Ulysses and Penelope' with Temple as they hurried away, Harry expresses his admiration for Ulysses and compares himself to Telemachus: 'He was in search of his father. He found him at last. Upon my honour, Temple, when I think of it, I'm ashamed to have waited so long.' Harry makes the comparison after several minutes of discussion. The reader who knows the Ulysses story can beat him to it and then, like him, see both his

9

past and his future in a new light. As he and his father meet and part, search for and miss each other, the Harry/Telemachus parallel confirms that his journeyings over land and sea are a special kind of quest.

These classical allusions do not jar, as they are compatible with earlier discussions which the young scholars have. But how many Victorian novel-readers would have known classical literature as well as Harry and Temple, or even have heard of Ulysses, Penelope and Telemachus? By incorporating such allusions in his novel, Meredith appears to have appealed to what Alton Locke called 'the few', rather than to 'the many' who read Crabbe, Burns, Wordsworth, Hood and Dickens (*Alton Locke*, 9). (Contemporary reviewers of Meredith's novels criticised them for their obscurity.) Alton could have been talking about most early- and mid-Victorian novelists when he said that 'there is an element especially democratic, truly levelling' in Tennyson's 'handling of the trivial everyday sights and sounds of nature'. Nevertheless, although these novelists provided much of the impetus behind the mid-century 'great tide' which set towards 'that which is common to the many', appealing to a large readership, many incorporated some allusions which could have been understood only by the kind of readers Dr Johnson had in mind in 1781, when he told Wilkes that there is 'community of mind' in quotation and that 'classical quotation is the *parole* of literary men all over the world'.[1] How is it, then, that quite different types and classes of Victorian readers, from learned literary men who shared 'community of mind' to people who relied on others to read to them, were often entertained by the same fiction, at least until the 1870s?

Whereas our most outstanding contemporary literary talents rarely challenge the popular thriller writers in the Top Ten sales lists for long, most of the best early- and mid-Victorian novelists, up to and including George Eliot, generally appealed to a wide range of readers by giving them what they wanted: novels of 'human interest', in the English 'realistic' tradition, having recognisably individual characters and (usually) credible and developed plots. Every reader, from the philosopher to the shop-girl, could share a common interest in how characters might respond to a new turn of events in the next episode of a current serial novel. Other aspects of many novels, however, must have appealed to the intellectuals but been ignored by the

shop-girls. For example, a discussion on some theological issue
of the day might crop up in an otherwise undemanding novel and
be passed over without losing one's grip on the plot. Similarly,
allusions in Victorian novels can at once have important functions, noticed by those who recognise them, and yet be ignored if
they are not recognised, because they themselves are dependent
for their effects upon their relationship to the main thematic or
plot lines of the novel, which can be followed without paying
attention to the allusions. Moreover, many allusions which have
an important function in a novel were easily recognisable, drawing on the literary classics with which the majority of readers
would have been familiar: the Authorised Version of the Bible,
the Book of Common Prayer, the *Pilgrim's Progress*, translations
of the *Arabian Nights*, and others. The foundations of most
early- and mid-Victorian novels were built on common ground
which was familiar to a wide range of mainly middle-class
readers.

Whether they noticed or ignored allusions, those readers
would probably not have dismissed them out of hand as annoy-
ing excrescences, as they were consciously or unconsciously
used to the constant casting and breaking of the 'spell' of realistic
fiction. Ask readers what they most like about such fiction and
they will probably mention their involvement in novels or their
inability to put them down. Most could recount experiences
similar to William George Clark's when reading *Jane Eyre*: 'as
we read on we forgot both commendations and criticism, identified ourselves with Jane in all her troubles, and finally married
Mr. Rochester about four in the morning.'[2] Our absorption in
fiction, however, is more usually only partial, like Glaucus's
engrossment in a book in Keats's *Endymion*:

> Strange matters did it treat of, and drew on
> My soul page after page, till *well-nigh* won
> Into forgetfulness.
> (III.679–81; my emphasis)

Clark could hurry through *Jane Eyre* at a sitting. The Brontës,
however, were the only major Victorian novelists who published
exclusively in volume form. The vast majority of novels were first
published in monthly parts or in serial form in the magazines and
only later went into volumes. Part or serial publication obviously

breaks up the narrative. Authorial intrusion has a similar effect, though more locally, when the omniscient novelist-narrator, familiar in the nineteenth century, casually introduces a personal statement. Kingsley took authorial intrusion to extremes when he inserted a long parenthetical passage in his first novel, *Yeast* (1848):

> But the truth was, Argemone thought herself infinitely superior to the colonel, for which simple reason she could not in the least understand him.
> [By the bye, how subtly Mr. Tennyson has embodied all this in *The Princess*. . . .]
> They said no more to each other that evening. (2)

Other features of Victorian fiction remind the reader that novelists conflate the real and the imaginary. Fictional characters inhabit a 'London' which is recognisably the real London. The more artificial devices of plotting, such as coincidence, are accepted as conventions which the writer is free to exploit in moderation. As Richard Stang has pointed out, by the mid-nineteenth century the idea that the novel was mere 'light escape literature' was usually regarded as outmoded.[3] Allusion was only one of several elements of Victorian fiction which drew attention to and often heightened the tension between the real and the imaginary which is one of its characteristics.

In order to ascertain how Victorian readers were likely to have responded to allusion in fiction, we need to consider the kinds of literary and non-literary quotations and references with which they were familiar and the habits of mind which would have made them receptive to allusion.

II

A dominant Victorian middle class offered writers a large and voracious reading public. Although a mature working-class sub-culture developed alongside the middle-class culture which is in fact what most of us think of as 'Victorianism', it is noticeable that working-class readers often emulated their social 'superiors' in their reading, partly through the influence of the institutes and clubs established by middle-class philanthropists.

(Similarly, many working-class poets wrote studiedly literary verse and eschewed the sub-culture of street balladry, penny dreadfuls and the halls.) What did Barbarians, Philistines and Populace alike see in the Philistine-dominated world around them which would have made them receptive to allusion in fiction?

Emerson's interpretation of 'quotation' as a symptom of a specifically American anxiety concerning the identity of the New World in relation to the Old can also be applied to certain aspects of the Victorians' response to the past:

> We do not believe our own thought; we must serve somebody; we must quote somebody; we dote on the old and the distant; we are tickled by great names; we import the religion of other nations; we quote their opinions; we cite their laws. . . . Thus we do not carry a counsel in our breasts, or do not know it; and because we cannot shake off from our shoes this dust of Europe and Asia, the world seems to be born old, society is under a spell, every man is a borrower and a mimic, life is theatrical, and literature a quotation; and hence that depression of spirits, that furrow of care, said to mark every American brow.
>
> 'Success', in *Society and Solitude* (1870). (*Works*, p. 472)

In England the syncretism of pre-Victorian architecture, typified in the contrast between the oriental Royal Pavilion at Brighton (1815–21) and the classical façade of the British Museum (1823–47), continued to be a feature of High Victorianism when the age had established its own architectural identity. The Gothic Revival of the late eighteenth century, itself 'alluding' to the medieval past, had a lasting influence on designers until late in the nineteenth century, with other movements going on alongside it. The Pre-Raphaelites breathed new life into artistic medievalism in the middle of the century, drawing on specific art-historical sources and often finding inspiration in Keatsian and Tennysonian historical settings. At the same time, Classicism ruled in the Academy and classical literary studies formed the backbone of education in the humanities. The retrospective tendency in the arts and education, whether Romantic Gothicism or Classicism, was expressed through various forms of reference to sources which were venerated for their intrinsic merits and for their longevity.

This respect for the past was symptomatic of the widely held belief that change in the century following the Industrial Revolution was too rapid and disruptive. An indication of this uneasiness in an age of rapid change was the apparently universal habit of hoarding and sharing inherited and contemporary wisdom from which a sense of moral and psychological security could be gained. The garnering of old saws and new apothegms was evident wherever one turned. The text embroidered on the sampler was displayed in a million parlours; churches and chapels had texts engraved in their stone porches or painted on walls and ceilings; tracts or short extracts from improving works were slipped into hands or pockets in the street, in an age in which cheap paper made it possible for the Evangelicals to be prodigal in their use of printed matter. Anthologies of extracts and quotations from literary and religious works sold in huge quantities. These were often arranged by topic so that the reader could dip into certain sections of, say, a collection of literary quotations for the kind of support or inspiration needed at any particular time. Edward Fitzgerald's *Polonius: A Collection of Wise Saws and Modern Instances* (1852) covered 'Quickness of Wit' with quotations ranging from the Classics through to Carlyle. The Hon. Mrs Lyttelton Gell offered nuggets of wisdom on 'The Canker of Self' from Marcus Aurelius, Mazzini and Plumptre, among others, in her popular *Cloud of Witness: A Daily Sequence of Great Thoughts from Many Minds, Following the Christian Seasons* (1891). Over fifty different books of selections and extracts from Shakespeare were compiled during the Victorian age, including *Religious and Moral Sentences Culled from the Works of Shakespeare* (1843), *Shakespeare's Household Words* (1859) and *Shakspeare for Schools: Being Passages from his Works to be Committed to Memory* (second edition, 1865). This last example was one of many expurgated literary texts which came into their own when English Literature became part of school syllabuses in the 1870s. Children were expected to memorise longer and longer passages of poetry each year and show a 'knowledge of meaning and allusions'.[4] The works of famous contemporary writers were also cannibalised. George Eliot's *Wise, Witty and Tender Sayings* appeared in 1872 and the *Sayings of Mrs. Humphry Ward* in 1915, eight and five years before their respective deaths. The most famous Victorian statement on literary extracts is Matthew Arnold's:

> There can be no more useful help for discovering what poetry belongs to the class of the truly excellent, and can therefore do us most good, than to have always in one's mind lines and expressions of the great masters, and to apply them as a touchstone to other poetry. . . . Short passages, even single lines, will serve our turn quite sufficiently.
>
> 'The Study of Poetry' (1880, as the Introduction to the *English Poets*)

Testing for the 'truly excellent' may have been one of the compilers' aims in *Polonius* and the Shakespeare anthologies, but many editors concentrated on amassing as many gnomic statements as possible, irrespective of their literary merits. And Arnold himself emphasised that the excellent does us 'most good'.

The quoting and compiling of clusters of texts was familiar enough to what Owen Chadwick calls the 'man in the pew'.[5] Of course, what the worshipper heard on Sundays depended largely on which pew he frequented. For example, in *Robert Elsmere* (1888) Mary Ward describes a 'Dissenting minister' who was probably typical in certain respects: he displays a 'gymnastic dexterity in the quoting and combining of texts' at which most Broad Churchmen would have scoffed (II.15). Some conventions, however, were common to almost all Christian sects. Novel readers who found a motto on the title-page would have been familiar with the kind of text which introduced the sermon in church or chapel, and which headed the printed sermons which were standard reading for Sundays. Thus they would have expected a title-page motto to be some sort of thematic pointer to what follows. In this respect, literary technique conforms to the aims of the many novelists who must have sympathised with Trollope's view of himself as a 'preacher of sermons', expounded in his *Autobiography* of 1883 (8). (Thackeray considered that his profession was 'as serious as the parson's own'.[6]) Daily Bible study and exegesis in the family circle, with key texts taken up in accompanying prayers; the familiar use of cross-references to texts in tracts, the marginalia of the *Pilgrim's Progress* and the Bible itself; and the often unconscious adoption of biblical words and phrases in normal discourse, all helped to make the use of biblical texts for illustrative purposes a habit of mind. At home and in his place of worship, the 'man in the pew' used allusion to support his views and to underpin his faith.

If habits of worship and Bible study had the greatest influence upon Victorians in their approach to allusion, the use of a knowledge of classical and modern literature to strengthen the sense of group identity shared by the better educated came a strong second. George Watson has shown that the Classics were a 'dying decoration to Victorian oratory' and that Gladstone's adherence to the convention of quoting the Classics in the House of Commons was seen as an anachronism.[7] Old habits died harder in other quarters, however, and people inside and outside the academic world used classical and modern literary allusion as a quantifier of learning and breeding throughout the Victorian age. The published version of Lord Acton's inaugural lecture on the study of history, delivered at Cambridge in 1895, included an appendix containing 105 quotations illustrating the 28 pages of his text. Although few of the quotations were from the Classics, they had the laboured effect of proving that Acton was very widely read. The same kind of litmus allusion is still with us. Source works now tend to be chosen from the classics of English literature, as obscure to many modern readers as Homer and Virgil were to all but the best educated Victorians. For example, *The Times*'s first leader for 6 December 1975 opened with a sentence in which quotation is the '*parole*' of '*Times* Readers' worthy of the name: 'In the late season of this year portents of disquiet have been "thick as autumnal leaves that strow the brooks in Vallombrosa."'

The use in normal discourse of easily recognisable quotations from such works as the Bible and the *Pilgrim's Progress* stands at the opposite end of the scale of allusion as display. Many of these allusions became part of the language, familiar and unremarkable. In *Far from the Madding Crowd* (1874), Gabriel Oak has a small, heterogeneous collection of books, as unpretentious as its owner:

> *The Young Man's Best Companion, The Farrier's Sure Guide, The Veterinary Surgeon, Paradise Lost, The Pilgrim's Progress, Robinson Crusoe*, Ash's *Dictionary*, and Walkingame's *Arithmetic*, constituted his library; and though a limited series, it was one from which he had acquired more sound

information by diligent perusal than many a man of opportunities has done from a furlong of laden shelves. (8)

Richard Altick explains that the cottager who preserved his 'little
shelf of worn and precious books, family possessions passed
down through a century or more – the Bible, *Robinson Crusoe*,
Pilgrim's Progress, ballads, and chapbooks', was one of a dying
breed: 'when the children moved to the cities, the books were left
behind or soon were lost in the course of their owners' restless
migration from one tenement to another, and there was little
chance to replace them' (Altick, p. 95). Elizabeth Gaskell, however, portrayed certain members of the Manchester working-
class of the 1830s and 1840s as avid readers in *Mary Barton*
(1848). Even where no other books were read, a few religious
works were to be found in all but the poorest homes, and in most
were opened on Sundays. In this way 'countless children acquired an intimate knowledge of *Paradise Lost* and *Pilgrim's
Progress* – books which they might never have known but for an
English Sunday' (Altick, p. 127). The two books which Altick
mentions here were the very ones which Macaulay claimed to
know by heart. A great novel addict, he would have been
admirably equipped to identify the thousands of quotations from
these works and the Bible in Victorian fiction. And some of his
servants probably read the same novels and identified at least the
more obvious of these allusions. One modern commentator
asserts that the 'intellectual attainments of most of the middle
and upper classes of Victorian England were not very impressive
by modern standards'.[8] Whereas the modern reader has greater
breadth of knowledge, however, the Victorian reader had a more
detailed familiarity with a few of the key works which formed the
literary corner-stone of the 'shared culture' of the age.

Modern readers of Victorian novels become increasingly
familiar with the spirit of the age and its received ideas as they
read. Trollope's claim that he could make his 'sermons' both
'salutary and agreeable' to his readers by portraying 'characters
like themselves, – or to which they might liken themselves'
(*Autobiography*, 8), strengthens the modern reader's feeling
that he has learnt as much about real Victorians as he has about
the fictional characters by the end of a Trollope novel. Similarly,
when examining allusions in Victorian fiction, and particularly
allusions which were easily recognisable, we will see that the

recurrence of certain adopted texts chosen by novelists, and of allusive techniques within the novels, tells us much about the relationship between the fiction and the age in which it was written. When I turn to the novels which are to be discussed in detail I will distinguish between allusions to familiar works such as the *Pilgrim's Progress*, arcane allusions which few Victorians would have recognised, and the many allusions which belong to an intermediate category, drawing on adopted texts which only the well read would have known or at least been able to look up, but which could not be described as arcane. In such an anti-quarian exercise, in which the modern reader tries to stand in the Victorian reader's shoes, the main pitfall is over-zealousness in research, whereby more comes to light than would have been obvious to even the widely read at the time of publication. One of my main aims is to show that some aspects of allusion in Victorian fiction, and particularly in the earlier novels I examine, invite readings which would have been more obvious to *many* of the first readers of the novels than they are to us today.

III

The allusions with which I will be concerned function mainly within three areas of reference: cultural, generic and textual. Cultural allusions help to identify or define national, regional or class cultures. Scott, whose influence on Victorian fiction was so great, established a sense of national identity in his novels through allusions to Scottish balladry and legend, as Hardy was to use Wessex allusions to define a specific regional culture later. Hardy incorporated a set of class-cultural allusions at the end of *Jude the Obscure* (1894–5), when the pathos of Jude's death is heightened by memories of his early aspirations. The sounds of an honorary degree ceremony float across to the Christminster room in which Jude lies in an open coffin:

The old, superseded, Delphin editions of Virgil and Horace, and the dog-eared Greek Testament on the neighbouring shelf, and the few other volumes of the sort that he had not parted with, roughened with stone-dust where he had been in the habit of catching them up for a few minutes between his labours, seemed to pale to a sickly cast at the sounds. (VI.11)

The right to the benefits of studying the kind of books to which Hardy refers belongs to the doctors who are conferring degrees and to the gentry who are receiving them, but not to a stonemason. Allusion marks the class barriers of Christminster.

Generic allusion indicates the relationship between an adoptive text and a literary convention or tradition. Scott followed the example of his eighteenth-century precursors when he explicitly stated how his *Waverley; or, 'Tis Sixty Years Since* (1814) should be placed in relation to novelistic tradition:

> Had I . . . announced in my frontispiece, 'Waverley, a Tale of other Days,' must not every novel-reader have anticipated a castle scarce less than that of Udolpho, of which the eastern wing had long been uninhabited, and the keys either lost, or consigned to the care of some aged butler or housekeeper, whose trembling steps, about the middle of the second volume, were doomed to guide the hero, or heroine, to the ruinous precincts? Would not the owl have shrieked and the cricket cried in my very title-page? (1)

He goes on to poke fun at German romance, the 'Sentimental Tale' and the high-society novel, thus defending his own work by means of attack, and partly answering the conscious or unconscious questions which we all ask when first opening a novel: to which literary conventions does this work conform, and what should I expect to find as I read? (It is often by working *against* such expectations later in the text that a writer can achieve his most powerful effects.)

Kenneth Moler has shown that Jane Austen's 'Art of Allusion' is mainly what I call 'generic' in emphasis. Moler suggests that in each of Austen's novels 'the manipulation of one or perhaps a combination of several traditional motifs, character types, situations, or themes constitutes an important part of the moral and intellectual substance, the "meaning," of the work as a whole', and that it is profitable to consider some of her 'borrowings' from the 'common stock' as 'things more nearly akin to "allusions," implied references that she expects to affect her audience'.[9] The vagueness of Moler's distinction between what he calls 'borrowings' and 'allusions' reflects the nature of the material he analyses, for Austen's 'borrowings' are often *'implicit* invitations to the reader to see relationships and make comparisons between

her works and what they resemble' [my emphasis]. I believe that
a distinction often can and should be made between the kind of
adaptive strategy adopted by Austen in her 'imitation, parody,
correction of her predecessors and contemporaries' (Moler,
p. 1), and the kinds of 'explicit' quotations and references in
Victorian fiction with which I am mainly concerned, and whose
importance seems to have been recognised by modern readers
less often than that of 'allusions' in Moler's sense. The distinction can, however, be difficult to make, as I show in my
discussion of *The Egoist* (Chapter 7), a novel in which Meredith
seems to tease the reader when offering him 'allusions' which are
sometimes closer to Moler's definition than to mine.

Textual allusions are by far the most common kind in Victorian fiction, establishing links between specific adopted and
adoptive texts. They fulfil one or more of four different types of
local function, which often complement each other. The first,
very common type of textual allusion in the fiction exemplifies
the Victorian habit of encapsulating and preserving wise sayings: the gnomic allusion, that is, a statement transcribed or
adapted in order to underline some message or theme economically. Allusion in the form of gnomic statements has always been
common in literature. Significantly, Richard Lanham's *Handlist
of Rhetorical Terms* (1968) lists no fewer than four terms which
could be applied to various kinds of gnomic allusion: *aenos* (the
quoting of wise sayings from fables), *apomnemonysis* (the
quoting of an approved authority from memory), *chria* (1. a
short exposition of a deed or saying of a person whose name is
mentioned), and *paroemia* (the quoting of proverbs). The identity of the author of the adopted text from which a gnomic allusion
is taken, and the context of the passage in the adopted text, are
often of little or no significance. Hardy's description of the advice
which Tess Durbeyfield should have heeded before she left home
suggests how widely such advice is disseminated: 'sundry
gnomic texts and phrases known to her and to the world in
general' (*Tess of the d'Urbervilles* (1891), 15). Once such texts
and phrases are shared by the world in general their sources are
sometimes obscured in the same way that folklore cannot always
be traced to specific regions and periods. The reader does not
need to be familiar with the adopted text of this inaccurate
gnomic quotation in *Tom Brown at Oxford* (1861): '"Do well
unto thyself and men will speak good of thee," is a maxim as old

as King David's time, and just as true now as it was then' (26). A knowledge of the original gnomic statement and its source is sometimes essential, however, especially when that statement has been changed in some way in the adoptive text. Trollope's gentle irony would not have been missed by the contemporary reader of *Framley Parsonage*: 'He had been poor enough then, and the duke had not treated him in the most courteous manner in the world. How hard it is for a rich man not to lean upon his riches! harder, indeed, than for a camel to go through the eye of a needle' (8).

Like gnomic allusions, the second type of textual allusion, which I will call shorthand notations, are conveniently concise, often being used to suggest typicality of character succinctly. Unlike many gnomic allusions, their effect depends entirely upon their recognition by the reader. *Framley Parsonage* again contains examples. Trollope explains that Lord Lufton enjoys flirting with the beautiful Griselda Grantly and that the flirtation seems doubly delightful because it makes Lufton's fellow nobleman, Lord Dumbello, intensely jealous. He continues: 'It must be remembered that our gallant, gay Lothario had passed some considerable number of days with Miss Grantly in his mother's house, and the danger of such contiguity must be remembered also.' Everything in this sentence suggests the intimate sharing of knowledge between writer and reader. The latter, it is implied, will be able to remember the specific fact that Lufton and Miss Grantly have been together, and, like Trollope himself, will remember the general truth that there is danger in such contiguity. Lufton is *'our* gallant, gay Lothario', the acquaintance of writer and reader alike. The reader is expected to know of Lothario as a proverbial type, even if the unmarked quotation from a famous line in Rowe's *The Fair Penitent* ('Is this that haughty, gallant, gay Lothario?') goes unnoticed. Like the general statement on the 'danger of such contiguity', the shorthand notation places Lufton against a familiar backdrop of typicality. Although biblical, Miss Dunstable's references to Lazarus in her discussion with Mrs Gresham are as flippant as the Lothario reference: 'You've learned to like London well enough since you sat down to the table of Dives. Your uncle, – he's the real impracticable, unapproachable Lazarus who declares that he can't come down because of the big gulf. I wonder how he'd behave, if somebody left him ten thousand a year?' (38). Miss

Dunstable blasphemes in the mildest way for comic effect. Otherwise the choice of Lazarus as a typical figure is merely a matter of convenience. Earlier in the same speech she makes an even less suggestive comparison, saying that Mrs Gresham is 'a weak little thing, by no means able to contend with such a Samson as Mrs Harold [Smith]'. In this third example the typical character referred to is merely a shorthand notation for the opposite of 'weak little thing', the ludicrous sex difference and the inappropriateness of the context belying the possibility of subtler parallels.

The third type of textual allusion is the borrowed embellishment, such as a purple passage or a reference which merely gives the (often false) impression that a writer is learned. The borrowing of a purple passage is often mere self-indulgence, associated with the kind of 'pleasure' which Anne Elliott found in her country walk in *Persuasion* (1818) 'from repeating to herself some few of the thousand poetical descriptions extant of autumn, that season of peculiar and inexhaustible influence on the mind of taste and tenderness, that season which has drawn from every poet, worthy of being read, some attempt at description, or some lines of feeling' (10). The authorship and context of such a passage are generally irrelevant. Allusions can be used to add a sophisticated touch to a piece of writing, as Bulwer's Mr Cleveland knew when he 'wanted to enrich one of his letters with a quotation from Ariosto, which he but imperfectly remembered', in *Alice* (1838; IV.3). Bulwer himself draws on a great writer when he quotes Wordsworth in *Eugene Aram* (1832):

> The heavens broadened round him in all the loving yet august tranquillity of the season and the hour; the stars bathed the living atmosphere with a solemn light; and above – about – around –
>> 'The holy time was quiet as a nun
>> Breathless with adoration.'
>
> He looked forth upon the deep and ineffable stillness of the night, and indulged the reflections that it suggested. (I.4)

The fourth type of textual allusion tends to be the most interesting and important: allusion as a plot pointer or thematic pointer in the adoptive text. In *Tess*, Alec d'Urberville whistles a line of 'Take, O take those lips away', but the 'allusion' is 'lost upon Tess' (9). For the reader who knows that the Boy sings this song for Mariana, seduced by Angelo and abandoned in her moated grange in *Measure for Measure*, Tess is seen to be pathetically ignorant of the irony of the allusion. This is an example of a plot pointer in the main text of a novel. The motto, prefacing a novel, or a book or chapter in a novel, often fulfils a similar function. When Kingsley used a quotation from Newman's *Sermons on the Theory of Religious Belief* as his motto for 'What, then, does Dr. Newman Mean?' (1864), Newman complimented him on his 'felicitous' thematic pointer in his reply, the *Apologia* of the same year: 'A motto should contain, as in a nutshell, the contents, or the character, or the drift, or the *animus* of the writing to which it is prefixed' (I). Title-page mottoes have been used in all kinds of English literature. The first of the two biblical mottoes which prefaced Milton's essay, the *Doctrine and Discipline of Divorce* (1643), served as an author's apology: 'MATT. xiii. 52. Every scribe instructed in the kingdom of heaven is like the master of a house, which bringeth out of his treasury things new and old.' The Latin quotation which prefaces Shelley's *Prometheus Unbound* (1820) draws attention to the poet's radical reshaping of a myth which he thought Aeschylus had weakened in his *Prometheia*.[10] T. S. Eliot helped to perpetuate the convention of the prefatory motto with his classical quotations heading *The Waste Land* (1922) and *Burnt Norton* (1935), and with the quotation from Conrad's *Heart of Darkness* in *The Hollow Men* (1925), which haunts the poem like a spectre: 'Mistah Kurtz – he dead.' Crabbe's use of mottoes in *The Borough* (1810) and the *Tales in Verse* (1812) was more unusual in poetic works. The individual Letters of *The Borough* are prefaced by quotations taken from classical authors, Shakespeare and various English poets. These mottoes are similar to the chapter mottoes which, particularly after Scott's rise to fame, became a familiar feature of the nineteenth-century novel. In the *Tales in Verse* each tale is prefaced by a number of quotations from Shakespeare. Although Crabbe probably revelled in the challenge of finding several quotations in Shakespeare which were relevant to each tale, this habit of searching the work of one writer for numerous suitable passages indicates an unimaginative approach to allusion. The best mottoes tend to stand alone and have a specific function in the novels, books or chapters which they preface.

Ann Radcliffe, who appears to have established the convention in the novel, added mottoes to *The Romance of the Forest* (1791), *The Mysteries of Udolpho* (1794) and *The Italian* (1797). Twelve of the mottoes in *The Italian* were chosen from the works of Shakespeare, the most popular source of mottoes in the Victorian novel. But by far the most prolific and influential writer and borrower of chapter mottoes was Walter Scott. Tom Haber has shown that 'Shakespere, as might be expected, is Scott's favorite source; from Shakespere Scott chose tags for 202 chapters – a number nearly twice as large as the total of "Old Play," "Old Song," and "Old Ballad" titles'.[11] Scott's habit of writing almost all the last mentioned mottoes himself, usually because he could not be bothered to look up suitable sources, was later adopted by some Victorian novelists, including Elizabeth Gaskell and George Eliot.

The best mottoes become integral parts of texts, generally functioning as crucial plot pointers or thematic pointers. As chapter mottoes and headings prepare the reader for what follows and, in the case of mottoes at least, are almost invariably inserted by the author himself, readers who ignore them miss what may be an important element of the text, particularly as partial knowledge of what is to follow adds to the tension generated by the development of a plot. Allusions in the main body of a text can have similar functions. We tend to read the early chapters of a novel more slowly than later ones, while we learn how to read the text which is new to us and try to place it in relation to various conventions. On finding allusions in these early chapters we are likely to attend to their potential significance in the novel as a whole. Esther Summerson's reading of the story of the woman taken in adultery in the third chapter of *Bleak House* (1852–3), which kills off her godmother, points to the guilty secret which emerges later in the novel. Charley Hexam's reference to the Flood in the third chapter of *Our Mutual Friend* (1864–5) complements Dickens's descriptions of the encroaching Thames in a novel which is dominated by the image of the great river. Allusions incorporated in the early or later chapters of novels can also indicate structural parallels between adopted (or, here, *parallel*) texts and adoptive texts. For example, numerous Victorian novels contain allusions to the *Pilgrim's Progress* which suggest that their heroes or heroines are on a kind of spiritual journey through life.

Many of the Victorian novels which are deservedly never read today are crammed with allusions. Mottoes proved to be good fillers of space for the weaker novelists when they were compelled to publish in the ubiquitous three-decker form. Allusions in the text are often no more than lumber incorporated for show. Elizabeth Gaskell wrote to one Herbert Grey after the publication of his novel, *The Three Paths* (1859): 'It was the want of a plot, – & the too great dwelling on feelings &c, – & the length of the conversations, which *did not advance the action* of the story, – & the too great reference to books &c – which only impede the narration – that appeared to me the prevalent faults in your book.'[12] As a writer who made frequent 'reference to books &c', Elizabeth Gaskell seems to have been aware that the use of allusion had to be justified by its function in the text.

IV

In all the novels under discussion in the following chapters the use of allusion is most certainly justified. Allusion helps to elucidate the meaning of each text and to indicate the literary modes and conventions in which its author works. For example, allusion underpins the central apocalyptic theme in *Hard Times*; parable is accommodated within a realistic narrative through allusion in *Mary Barton*.

The Victorian reader who brought his knowledge of literature and the Bible and his familiarity with various kinds of allusion to his reading of contemporary fiction was partly fulfilling his side of what I will call the 'reader-narrator contract'. Most Victorian novels are narrated in the third-person voice by what is assumed to be an author-narrator. Being 'omniscient', this narrator implicitly contracts to supply the reader with the information he needs in order to understand plot and character by describing people's points of view, introducing dialogues with explanatory comments, linking various sections of his narrative through symbolism, and so on. Autobiographical narrators make a contract with the reader which is also generally honoured by the end of the novel, but which differs from that of the omniscient narrator in some ways, being narrower in scope. Allusion is one of several means by which these reader-narrator contracts are

sealed. We will see that the 'Reader' in *Jane Eyre*, directly
addressed by Jane as she writes her autobiography, is privileged
to be well informed and thus to feel comparatively secure as he
assimilates a controlled flow of data concerning her past. Jane
honours the implicit contract of the autobiographer with her
reader, reconstructing her past in the form of a straightforwardly
sequential narrative, apparently giving him all he needs to
satisfy his curiosity and allowing little to go unexplained. Allusion helps the reader to understand the novel by providing fixed
points on the map of Jane's journey through life. Whereas *Jane
Eyre* was highly regarded by Victorian readers and critics,
Wuthering Heights was generally considered to be a 'rude and
strange production', as Charlotte Brontë described it in her
preface of 1850. Nowadays the positions are reversed, with
Emily's elusive masterpiece judged to be a far greater novel than
Jane Eyre by the majority of critics. In *Wuthering Heights* the
ambiguities of the implicit contract between reader and narrators
are reflected in the use of allusion in the narrative. Of the very
few allusions in the novel, one is of crucial importance: the text of
Branderham's sermon ('Seventy Times Seven') which Lockwood
reads in the coffin-bed before he has his nightmares (3). Preceding the main retrospective narrative which begins in chapter 4,
the cluster of clues which Lockwood tries to decipher, including
the biblical allusion, teaches the reader how to read a claustrophobic novel which generally refers only to itself. The allusion
is an ambiguous thematic pointer in an ambiguous novel.[13]

Unlike *Wuthering Heights*, many of the other Victorian novels
which are still read and admired today contain sets of related
allusions which help to define patterns or structures as important
as those of plot and symbolism. Until the last quarter of the
nineteenth century, when Meredith and Hardy narrowed the
scope of the reader-narrator contract, using allusion in more
obscure ways than their precursors, these sets of allusions were
usually drawn from adopted texts which were part of the 'shared
culture' mentioned earlier, thus being familiar to most Victorian
readers if not to many of their modern descendants. Victorian
novelists, including Meredith and Hardy, developed themes and
images, plot motifs and the portrayal of character around clusters of quotations and references. The novels discussed in the
following chapters range widely in type and in their dates of
publication, yet each contains sets of allusions which are used in
these ways.

3

The Heroine as Reader: *Jane Eyre*

I

As Fanny Ratchford showed in her study of the Brontës' 'Web of Childhood' (1941), close analysis of Charlotte's juvenilia reveals much about her early reading and the influence of literary sources on her writings. However, Charlotte Brontë's early work is devoid of literary and biblical allusions which have an important function in their adoptive texts. Even in her later Angrian novelettes, most literary allusions are shorthand notations through which she merely classifies characters or makes some general comment on them. Their use is always local, having no pervasive controlling effect in the texts. The years between the 'Farewell to Angria', written in her diary late in 1839, and the completion of the fair copy of *The Professor* in June 1846 marked a period of personal and literary maturing for Charlotte Brontë, during which she had to cope with the stress which resulted from her experiences at the Pensionnat Heger and from Branwell's self-destructive behaviour at home in Haworth. Although *The Professor* was rejected by six publishers in 1846–7 and was not in fact published until after her death, in 1857, she wrote a new preface for the novel soon after the publication of *Shirley* in October 1849. She underlined a change of emphasis in her writing: 'I had not indeed published anything before I commenced *The Professor*, but in many a crude effort, destroyed almost as soon as composed, I had got over any such taste as I might once have had for ornamented and redundant composition, and come to prefer what was plain and homely' (Preface). William Crimsworth is the plain, homely and rather dull narrator of his own story. Two features of *The Professor* make it difficult for the reader to respond to or even acknowledge Crimsworth as the narrator. First, the preface and Crimsworth's own thoughts on his narrative are too similar. Thus Charlotte Brontë blurs the distinction between author and autobiographical narrator. Secondly, Crimsworth does not share Jane Eyre's strength of character, and therefore lacks the kind of individual narrative style with which she rivets her reader's attention in the later novel. The biographical school of critics point to Charlotte Brontë's reversal of the sexes in the pupil-teacher relationship which she shared with Heger as the main reason for Crimsworth's anaemia as a narrator, and thus also explain the greater strength of *Villette*, narrated by Lucy Snowe. All that concerns us here is the fact that Crimsworth is never strongly established as a retrospective narrator who can be imagined selecting key moments from his past, commenting on earlier events in the wisdom of his maturity, and quoting from or referring to literature and the Bible in his own way. It is sometimes Charlotte Brontë rather than Crimsworth who seems to be choosing the allusions which are incorporated in the text. But although the comparative shallowness of Crimsworth as a character, and thus as a narrator, makes his use of allusion less effective and convincing than Jane Eyre's, the development of a network of biblical and Bunyanesque allusions in *The Professor* indicates a technical advance on the juvenilia and a step towards the more sophisticated narrative and allusive methods of *Jane Eyre* (1847).

In the short final chapter ('Conclusion') of her autobiography, Jane intimates that she has been 'married ten years'. By the end of the narrative, then, her reader knows that the story of her journey through life, divided into five stages and suggestive of Christian 'progress' analogues, has been told by a traveller who has at last reached her destination at Ferndean, her true home, as Rochester's devoted wife. As the narrator of her own journey, she recalls those incidents and impressions along the route which strike her as important. Chapter 10 opens with an assessment of her role as narrator which could also be described as a clause in the reader-narrator contract, delimiting the areas which she is going to cover: 'Hitherto I have recorded in detail the events of my insignificant existence: to the first ten years of my life, I have given almost as many chapters. But this is not to be a regular autobiography: I am only *bound* to invoke memory where I know her responses will possess some degree of interest' (my emphasis). This statement on the perennial problem of selection, familiar even to the writer of the 'regular autobiography', strengthens one's trust in Jane as the sensible, self-critical narrator of her own story who has the uniquely intimate knowledge of the autobiographer. As she recalls her past, Jane often shows how she herself interprets or interpreted books, locations and human behaviour. Her early reading of literature and the Bible prepares her for problems of interpretation which she encounters when trying to analyse Rochester and Rivers at Thornfield and Moor House, and particularly when she has to analyse Rochester's famous cry. Meanwhile she is scrutinised by Brocklehurst, Rochester and Rivers. The heroine who describes herself as a 'reader' of people is 'read' herself.

II

Looking back on her early life at Gateshead-hall, Jane comments on Mrs Reed's position as an aunt who has been forced to adopt her: 'It must have been most irksome to find herself bound by a hard-wrung pledge to stand in the stead of a parent to a strange child she could not love, and to see an uncongenial *alien* permanently intruded on her own family group' (2; my emphasis). When she lives with the Reeds, Jane's sense of alienation is reflected in her response to her favourite books. Perusing the more sombre vignettes in the second volume of Thomas Bewick's *History of British Birds* (1804) makes Jane 'happy' in her own way as she sits hidden in the window-seat at the beginning of the novel (1). The many Victorian readers of *Jane Eyre* who knew Bewick's classic must have found her choice of illustrations as strange as the child herself. She concentrates on gloomy vignettes, such as the 'broken boat stranded on a desolate coast' and the 'quite solitary church-yard with its inscribed headstone', rather than the large plates of sea birds which enrich the second volume. Jane's enjoyment in studying desolate scenes is short-lived, as John Reed seizes the book and flings it at her, causing her to cut her head against the door. When she visits her dying aunt years later Jane notices the 'two volumes of Bewick's British Birds occupying their old place on the third shelf' and sketches

'fancy vignettes' which suggest that their spell is still potent: 'a
glimpse of sea between two rocks; the rising moon, and a ship
crossing its disk'(21). After the Red Room incident, Jane asks
Bessie to fetch *Gulliver's Travels* from the library (3). The
imaginary world of 'the little fields, houses, and trees, the
diminutive people, the tiny cows' of Lilliput, and the 'monster
cats, the tower-like men and women' of Brobdir.., ag, which has
formerly delighted her, now seems grotesque and horrifying:
'the giants were gaunt goblins, the pigmies malevolent and
fearful imps, Gulliver a most desolate wanderer in most dread
and dangerous regions.' After her interview with Brocklehurst
she takes a book, 'some Arabian tales', and finds that she can
'make no sense of the subject' as her own thoughts 'swim'
between herself and the page she has usually found fascinating
(4).

These early chapters should be a *locus classicus* for the child
psychologist. Jane's responses to her favourite books are directly
attributable to obsessions and anxieties which are engendered in
a hostile environment. But whereas she reinterprets *Gulliver's
Travels* with a disturbing rapidity, the adults who control her life
are confident that their own interpretations of scripture and of
moral law are definitive and should therefore be pressed upon the
child in their charge. Mrs Reed and Brocklehurst share hardened
prejudices and narrow *idées fixes* on which Jane is expected to
base her own judgments.

The contrast between the child and the adults who surround
her is heightened in Jane's interview with Brocklehurst. When
Brocklehurst arrives at Gateshead-hall he questions her in a
manner reminiscent of the liturgical Catechism and the kind of
dialogues which filled improving books in the nineteenth century, and presents her with a copy of the 'Child's Guide',
drawing her attention to 'that part containing "an account of the
awfully sudden death of Martha G——, a naughty child ad-
dicted to falsehood and deceit"'(4). The catechistic dialogue and
the 'Child's Guide' complement one another in the parodic
portrayal of Brocklehurst, who is presented as a *type* of clergyman, fearful to the young Jane but verging on the ridiculous to
the adult woman. The gap which yawns between the young
heroine's view of life and that of Brocklehurst's model child is
indicated by specific references to Jane's favourite books in the
Bible: 'Revelations [sic] and the book of Daniel, and Genesis and

Samuel, and a little bit of Exodus, and some parts of Kings and Chronicles, and Job and Jonah.' To Brocklehurst's dismay, she dislikes the Psalms, presumably because of their lack of plot, whereas his own 'little boy' knows six Psalms by heart and claims that he prefers learning a verse of a Psalm to eating a 'gingerbread-nut', thereby earning 'two nuts in recompense for his infant piety'. As a retrospective narrator, the adult Jane portrays Brocklehurst and his boy as representatives of types which would have been recognised instantly by a Victorian reader, but makes her own inner life, and specifically her early recognition of the differences between her own views and criteria and those of the people in authority over her, as tangible and individual as her impression of Brocklehurst as a 'black pillar' standing on the hearth-rug in the breakfast-room at Gateshead-hall.

When young Jane is sent to Lowood school her sense of alienation intensifies. On her arrival she tries to decipher the kind of clues which we all look for in a new place. She looks round the 'convent-like garden, and then up at the house; a large building, half of which seemed gray and old, the other half quite new' (5). As her eye travels across the new part of the building, her 'reading' of the house changes from the metaphorical to the literal, for she notices and is puzzled by a 'stone-tablet over the door' which bears an inscription: '"Lowood Institution. – This portion was rebuilt A.D.——, by Naomi Brocklehurst, of Brocklehurst Hall, in this county." "Let your light so shine before men that they may see your good works, and glorify your Father which is in heaven." – St. Matt. v. 16.' The inscription is both referentially specific and generically typical, being self-advertisement of the kind which can still be seen on nineteenth-century public buildings. The marked gnomic quotation from the Sermon on the Mount clearly indicates the nature of the lady whose name appears in the inscription, and introduces a theme which is to be developed in the Lowood chapters. One of the main strengths of *Jane Eyre* lies in the interdependence of physical and spiritual concerns throughout the autobiography. Having sick-ened over Jane's burnt porridge with her, the reader now joins her in 'pondering the signification of "Institution," and en-deavouring to make out a connection between the first words and the verse of scripture'. But of course, the adult reader, like the adult Jane, can make more of things which young Jane perceives than she herself can at the time. When her speculations on the inscription are interrupted by Helen Burns's cough, Jane sees that she is reading a book called *Rasselas* which looks 'dull' to her 'trifling taste': 'I saw nothing about fairies, nothing about genii; no bright variety seemed spread over the closely printed pages.' Unlike the innocent Jane, the reader can see the irony in the juxtaposition of the hypocritical inscription (appearance) and Johnson's *Rasselas* (reality), in which human life is said to be 'every where a state in which much is to be endured, and little to be enjoyed' (11).

After the typhus fever epidemic at Lowood, the school is moved to a more convenient building, where it is run by 'gentlemen of rather more enlarged and sympathizing minds' than Brocklehurst's (10). Jane spends eight more years at the school, six as a pupil and two as a teacher, during which time she takes advantage of 'an excellent education' but never ventures beyond the hills which surround the school. She then makes her first independent decision: to leave Lowood and become a private governess. Once beyond the hills, Jane has no Miss Temple on whom she can rely for advice. In place of the closed world of Lowood and the narrow but predictable Brocklehurst, Jane has Thornfield as a home and Rochester as a master. Both are to withhold their secret from her. During his first long dialogue with Jane at Thornfield, Rochester himself predicts that she will go through a period of transition:

> The Lowood constraint still clings to you somewhat; controlling your features, muffling your voice, and restricting your limbs; and you fear in the presence of a man and a brother – or father, or master, or what you will – to smile too gaily, speak too freely, or move too quickly: but in time, I think you will learn to be natural with me, as I find it impossible to be conventional with you; and then your looks and movements will have more vivacity and variety than they dare offer now.(14)

Rochester knows that he and Brocklehurst are poles apart in their attitudes and beliefs. Brocklehurst abominates natural behaviour and encourages the suppression of the instincts ('controlling', 'muffling', 'restricting'). Rochester rejects the constraints of convention and encourages natural behaviour ('smile

gaily', 'speak freely', 'move quickly'). Jane at least knew where
she was with Brocklehurst, however: in his catechistic interroga-
tions he was trying to determine whether his charge was de-
stined for heaven or hell; he was text-centred in everything that
he did, referring to the Bible as an unambiguous set of rules.
Rochester, on the other hand, initiates dialogues with Jane which
are catechistic in form and yet playful in tone. He is searching for
the unique, natural Jane, the Jane who has been hemmed in
hitherto by laws and conventions. Wanting to expose the natural
self in Jane and others, he devises means by which to test them
while himself remaining disguised. As in his dialogues, he plays
with conventions in order to catch people unawares.

Rochester is most devious in his methods of scrutiny when he
has a house-party staying at Thornfield (18). Jane examines
Miss Ingram in her usual way, watching her closely as she talks
with her friends or lounges on the sofa: 'I read daily in her a
proud security in [Rochester's] intentions respecting her.' Jane
uses the word 'read' in this way several times in the novel,
meaning 'to make out the character or nature of (a person, the
heart, etc.) by scrutiny or interpretation of outward signs' (*read*,
5d, *OED*). She is not alone in her reading: 'Other eyes besides
mine watched these manifestations of character. . . . Mr.
Rochester himself . . . exercised over his intended a ceaseless
surveillance.' Unlike Jane, however, Rochester uses indirect as
well as direct methods of surveillance. First he exploits the
possibilities offered him by a game of charades, entering into the
spirit of the theatricals by arranging elaborate sets, taking the
role, or disguise, of Miss Ingram's groom in order to enact
'bride', and playing Eliezer to her Rebecca for 'well'. Within
earshot of Jane he remarks to his acting partner after the scenes,
'remember you are my wife: we were married an hour since, in
the presence of all these witnesses'. Miss Ingram giggles and
blushes while Jane looks on. Rochester has manoeuvred every-
body in the room into the role of interpreter of his own and Miss
Ingram's motives and feelings through this 'pantomime of a
marriage'. Both Miss Ingram and Jane are scrutinised again
when he disguises himself as an old gipsy fortune-teller. Miss
Ingram returns from her consultation thoroughly displeased
with what she has heard. When Jane goes into the Library,
Rochester examines her face rather than her hand, rejecting
palmistry for phrenology and thus reversing the roles which each

played earlier in the novel when Jane examined his head (14). Rochester constantly presents Jane with new challenges as he experiments, now with the histrionic, now with the scientific, and as he shifts from mode to mode in conversation, now talking of fairies, now sounding like a Byronic hero in distress. He is attracted to Jane partly because she is so quick to take up the hints he gives her in the fast-moving battle of wits which develops between them, and it is during these dialogues that Jane tries to 'read' her master.

Her first opportunity of analysing Rochester's character comes when he invites her to talk with him in his 'after-dinner mood' (14). He asks her to draw her chair closer to him, so that he can see her clearly. Noticing that her gaze is 'fastened on his physiognomy', he asks her to 'criticize' him: 'He lifted up the sable waves of hair which lay horizontally over his brow, and showed a solid enough mass of intellectual organs; but an abrupt deficiency where the suave sign of benevolence should have risen.' Rochester invites the phrenological examination but is relieved when Jane's 'searching eyes' are turned away from him. Numerous references to these eyes confirm that she is a keen observer and interpreter of human behaviour. (Later in the novel, while Rochester waits impatiently for an answer to his proposal of marriage in the moonlit garden, Jane calmly asks him to turn his face so that she can 'read' his 'countenance' (23; my emphasis).)

Having offered his head for phrenological analysis, Rochester presents Jane with another set of clues, this time in the form of literary allusions. He hints at past sins: 'take my word for it, – I am not a villain: you are not to suppose that – not to attribute to me any such bad eminence; but . . . I am a trite common-place sinner.' This apparently casual unmarked quotation from Milton's description of Satan enthroned in hell, 'by merit raised/To that bad eminence' (*Paradise Lost*, II.5-6), is then followed up by Rochester in a way which suggests that he does in fact see himself as a sinner of epic proportions. Like Byron's heroes', his self-pity is reminiscent of Satan's: 'I could reform . . . but where is the use of thinking of it, hampered, burdened, cursed as I am?' A stronger verbal echo of *Paradise Lost* follows when Rochester talks of a 'fallen seraph of the abyss'. The educated Jane Eyre picks up these echoes and quotes Milton herself when she says to Rochester: 'You intimated that to have a sullied memory was a perpetual bane' (cf.I.692). In a kind of verbal tennis game, Rochester develops the allusion, quoting the lines which follow: 'as much better as pure ore is than foul dross' (cf.I.703-4). Before quoting Milton herself, Jane has told Rochester that she cannot 'keep up the conversation' as it has 'got out of [her] depth'. The famous description of the fallen angels in hell now provides common ground on which Jane and Rochester can meet, even though she probably first read *Paradise Lost* as a Puritan poem, whereas Rochester seems to read it in the spirit of Blake and Shelley, as a study of that Romantic hero, Satan. The reader who recognises these allusions becomes involved in Jane's attempts to analyse Rochester, who offers no more than clues to his inner self. Typically, his Miltonic allusions and hints of his own sinfulness are half-mocking, half-serious, leaving both Jane and the reader uncertain how to interpret his speeches.

Unlike Jane's readings of Gateshead-hall and Lowood, her impressions of Thornfield are contradictory. The house seems to be as ambiguous as its master. It is when she is shown over the house by Mrs Fairfax that she first hears the mysterious laugh emanating from one of the rooms off the long passage on the third storey (11). She describes this passage as 'narrow, low, and dim, with only one little window at the far end, and looking, with its two rows of small black doors all shut, like a corridor in some Bluebeard's castle'. Ironically, of course, Thornfield is more of a Bluebeard's castle than Jane at first suspects. This Bluebeard reference and the *Paradise Lost* quotations in chapter 14 are pointers to what follows in subsequent Thornfield chapters. Jane's impression of the house as a Bluebeard's castle with Gothic trimmings, intensified on the night before her wedding when Bertha Mason visits her bedroom (25), is held in tension with her view of the house and its grounds as an Eden. Having been given the clue at the beginning of chapter 23 that the orchard at Thornfield is 'Eden-like', most Victorian readers of the novel, being better educated than many of those who made up Dickens's wider readership, would have had little difficulty in recognising the numerous parallels to and quotations from Genesis and the fourth book of *Paradise Lost* which follow. The splitting of the horse-chestnut by lightning on the night after the betrothal in the garden suggests that Rochester is a fallen Adam, as it is reminiscent of the response of Nature to Adam's plucking of the fruit in *Paradise Lost*, the first thunderstorm (IX.1002). In

her description of herself leaving Thornfield after the Bertha
Mason revelations, Jane echoes Milton's description of the ex-
pulsion of Adam and Eve from Paradise in an unmarked quotation: 'I was weeping wildly as I walked along my solitary way'
(27; cf. *Paradise Lost*, XII.645–9). She and Rochester can meet
again only in a fallen world.

Both characters go through a long period of purgation and
soul-searching before they find the nearest possible approach to
Paradise in their fallen state at Ferndean. After their betrothal,
the narrative bristles with omens which complement the splitting
of the horse-chestnut. Jane's own doubts concerning her forthcoming marriage are based on her past experiences: 'Human
beings never enjoy complete happiness in this world. I was not
born for a different destiny to the rest of my species' (24). When
Rochester talks of Jane's power over him, she smilingly refers to
'Hercules and Samson with their charmers'. Following their
earlier Miltonic dialogue, Jane's thoughts are ominously appropriate, as Samson is typologically juxtaposed with Adam
when the latter rises from his 'amorous play' with Eve immediately after the Fall:

> So rose the Danite strong,
> Herculean Samson, from the harlot-lap
> Of Philistéan Dálilah, and waked
> Shorn of his strength.
>
> (IX.1059–62)

Jane's forebodings, her apparently casual allusion and her
dream of the ruined house (25) prove to be prophetic when
Rochester is injured in the fire at Thornfield and retreats to
Ferndean a temporarily blinded, semi-invalid Samson.

Other pointers in the betrothal chapters demand closer attention, being a set of allusions which establish an adopted text
(*Pilgrim's Progress*) as a parallel text.[1] But before looking at
these allusions, we must retrace our steps for a moment.

I find the first strong verbal echo of the *Progress* in the Lowood
chapters, when Jane relates how Miss Temple cleared her of the
charge of lying levelled at her by Brocklehurst: 'Thus relieved of
a grievous load, I from that hour set to work afresh, resolved to
pioneer my way through every difficulty: I toiled hard, and my
success was proportionate to my efforts' (8). Strongly reminis-

cent of Crimsworth's *Progress* allusions in *The Professor*, this statement is suggestive only of workaday endeavour. Wherever the reader finds the first echoes of the *Progress*, Jane's sense of alienation at the Reeds', her journey to Lowood, her discussions with Helen Burns and Miss Temple, those characters' allegorical names, Brocklehurst's antagonistic attitude towards her, and the physical hardships of the school all suggest parallels with Christian's story when reviewed with the *Progress* in mind. Allusions in fiction often have this kind of retroactive function, similar to that of a new clue in a detective story which changes all the evidence which the reader has amassed hitherto.

In the Thornfield and later chapters of the novel, the *Progress* has to be constantly borne in mind as a parallel text, and this influences the way in which Jane's autobiography is read. Rochester warns Jane that she would be taking on a 'useless burden' (24) if he were to tell her all his confidences. In the first of her pre-wedding dreams, Jane sees herself 'burdened with the charge of a little child', walking along a winding road in a storm (25). The description of the second dream also contains an echo of the *Progress*: Jane wanders among the ruins of Thornfield still carrying 'the unknown little child', being somehow unable to lay it down anywhere, however much it impedes her 'progress' (25). Stylistic clues are supported by obvious parallelism in the final paragraph of the second volume (chapter 26), when Jane is overcome with despair after the revelations of the wedding-day: 'The whole consciousness of my life lorn, my love lost, my hope quenched, my faith death-struck, swayed full and mighty above me in one sullen mass. That bitter hour cannot be described: in truth, "the waters came into my soul; I sank in deep mire: I felt no standing; I came into deep waters; the floods overflowed me."' Jane's marked quotation from Psalms 69.1-2 is similar in context to Bunyan's description of the Pilgrims entering the River of Death, in which he reworks the verses of the Psalm:

Then they asked the men, if the Waters were all of a depth? They said, No; yet they could not help them in that Case, for said they: *You shall find it deeper or shallower, as you believe in the King of the place.*
They then addressed themselves to the Water; and entring, *Christian* began to sink, and crying out to his good friend *Hopeful* he said, I sink in deep Waters, the Billows go over my

head, all his Waves go over me, *Selah.*

Then said the other, Be of good cheer, my Brother, I feel the bottom, and it is good. (Part I)

In the opening chapters of volume III, Jane describes her escape from Thornfield, mapping her route (physical and spiritual) with a Bunyanesque attention to analogical detail. Chapter 27 opens with self-questioning which is reminiscent of Christian's: 'What am I to do?' When the reply, 'Leave Thornfield at once', comes promptly, a battle is waged between conscience and passion: 'conscience, turned tyrant, held passion by the throat, told her, tauntingly, she had yet but dipped her dainty foot in the slough, and swore that with that arm of iron, he would thrust her down to unsounded depths of agony.' After Rochester's narrative of his past life and his intuition that Jane has previously seen a 'rough track' which she would have to travel, rather than living in the 'green flowery Eden' of his own imagination (27), she escapes from Thornfield at dawn and takes a coach to an area unfamiliar to herself and, she hopes, to Rochester. When dropped at Whitcross, 'absolutely destitute', her first task is Christian's: to decide the road she should take, in her case 'where four roads meet' (28). Sleeping in the open on heathland, Jane seems closer to God and to Nature than ever before. As in the *Progress*, personification suggests close contact between the traveller and those he meets: 'Night was come, and her planets were risen'; 'next day, Want came to me, pale and bare'. She wishes she had died in the night but sees that she still bears the responsibilities of being alive: 'The burden must be carried; the want provided for; the suffering endured; the responsibility fulfilled. I set out.'

Describing herself wandering through her version of the Valley of Humiliation, where she begs for crusts, and for food rejected by a pig, Jane seems to be rewriting the *Progress* for her own generation, both thematically, in her fall from governess to beggar, and stylistically, in her recasting of the biblical and Bunyanesque phraseology of the spiritual journey: 'Renewing, then, my courage, and gathering my feeble remains of strength, I pushed on'; 'I turned my face again to the village'; 'I had, by cross-ways and by-paths, once more drawn near the tracts of moorland'; 'I sank down where I stood, and hid my face against the ground' (28). The features of the landscape which Jane comes across are specifically Bunyanesque, though not encountered in the same sequence as in the *Progress*, when she walks towards the light shining on the moor. First, she is led over a hill. She then crosses a 'wide bog' where she falls twice, but is encouraged to continue by the light. She follows a 'road' or 'track' up to a 'wicket', and enters the garden of Moor House. The house is strongly reminiscent of the Palace Beautiful. She peers in at the Rivers girls through the window: 'Two young, graceful women – ladies in every point.' Although not beautiful they are 'grave', like Discretion in the Palace. Hannah the maid is less accommodating than Watchful the Porter; indeed, she is almost as threatening as the lions Christian meets. Once in the house, Jane is questioned about her journey, as Prudence, Piety, and Charity 'discourse' with Christian about his journey. That night, Jane thanks God for leading her to this hospitable place and falls asleep in her 'warm, dry bed'. Christian says to his hosts: 'Now I thank God I am here, and I thank you for receiving of me.'

This sequence of *Progress* analogues suggests that Jane has strayed from the narrow way at Thornfield. Before Rochester's secret is made public at the wedding, she enjoys the company of her beloved master and allows her emotions full rein. But once the secret is out, the severer side of her character, nurtured at Gateshead-hall and Lowood, reasserts itself. The voice of conscience tells her that passion has ruled her at Thornfield. She must pass through the Valley of Humiliation before she can arrive at the Palace Beautiful, whence she can perhaps proceed to the Celestial City. Leaving Rochester's domain, she falls into a strictly allegorical reading of landscape; it is as if Bunyan's Interpreter were describing her journey. And Moor House is inhabited by one who seems to offer her a direct route to the Celestial City. Her response to St John Rivers, however, proves to be more complex than such a simple pattern will allow.

Once she has settled into her new home, Jane finds Diana and Mary Rivers boon companions, but is puzzled and hurt by the coldness of their brother. Unlike Rochester, Rivers has a single purpose in life which makes everything that does not aid him in his purpose seem trivial. Jane and her female cousins draw and paint, read broadly, and study German. When Jane makes improvements to the house, Mary and Diana share in the pleasure this gives her (34). Rivers, on the other hand, thinks all such activities a waste of time, and keeps his eyes on his carefully chosen books, reading even during meals. He persuades Jane to give up German for 'Hindostanee', explaining that it will help him to have a pupil in the language which he is mastering in preparation for his missionary work. When Jane resists the pressure he puts on her to join him in this work, claiming that she has no vocation, he talks to her in the style of a practised preacher, seasoned with biblical texts:

'With St. Paul I acknowledge myself the chiefest of sinners: but I do not suffer this sense of my personal vileness to daunt me. I know my Leader: that He is just as well as mighty; and while He has chosen a feeble instrument to perform a great task, He will, from the boundless stores of His providence, supply the inadequacy of the means to the end. Think like me, Jane – trust like me. It is the Rock of Ages I ask you to lean on: do not doubt but it will bear the weight of your human weakness.' (34; cf. I Timothy 1.15, Philippians 3.21, Isaiah 26.4 (marginalia).)

He sees Jane and himself as apostles working towards a new heaven and a new earth, achieved through Pauline self-denial. He is a more subtle, more attractive Brocklehurst. Jane describes him as a 'cold cumbrous column' (34), reminiscent of the 'black pillar' on the hearth-rug at Gateshead-hall (4). Both men preach 'evangelical charity', both quote the famous 'fire and brimstone' text to Jane (Revelation 21.8), and both, like Paul, consider the body to be 'vile', advocating the suppression of nature (7, 29; 4, 35; 7, 34; 7, 31.) At Lowood, the resilient young Jane did not break down under the pressure which Brocklehurst brought to bear on her. At Moor House, however, she weakens as the more intelligent Rivers's will strengthens. She expresses her fears to him in terms which are reminiscent of Bunyan's allegory: 'My mind is at this moment like a rayless dungeon, with one shrinking fear fettered in its depths – the fear of being persuaded by you to attempt what I cannot accomplish' (34). She then seems to escape from this 'Doubting Castle' and decides to submit to Rivers's will. She is soon, however, to be thrown into fresh doubt, reminiscent of earlier moments of choice at life's crossroads.

Rivers finally brings the battle of wills between himself and Jane to a climax when he gives her a fortnight in which to decide whether she will be his wife and join him in India (35). Having rejected the broad way to destruction as Rochester's mistress, she now has to decide whether to follow the narrow way of this Evangelist (31,35). Rivers places his hands on her head, literally 'pressing' on her as if claiming her. She prays to Heaven: 'Shew me – shew me the path!' After a moment's silence she hears the uncanny cry from the distant Rochester: 'Jane! Jane! Jane!' (35). Rivers does not hear the cry and now has no power over her, failing to restrain her as she rushes into the garden. It is her turn to 'assume ascendancy': '*My* powers were in play, and in force.' All her earlier readings of her surroundings, and of the people who have tried to dominate her, have prepared Jane for this crucial moment of interpretation. Instinct, tempered with scepticism and balanced judgment developed at Gateshead-hall, Lowood and Thornfield, combine to guide her in her reading of the cry: '"Down superstition!" I commented, as that spectre rose up black by the black yew at the gate. "This is not thy deception, nor thy witchcraft: it is the work of nature. She was roused, and did – no miracle – but her best."' 'Superstition', 'witchcraft' and 'miracle' belie both the Gothic reading of things-which-go-bump-in-the-night at Thornfield, now exorcised by the revelation of the truth concerning Bertha Mason, and the scripture-based reading which Rivers might have supplied. Jane implicitly rejects the literary archetypes and religious formulae on which her sensibilities have been nurtured, recognising Nature as the agent of her liberation from the suppressive forces of her past. Instinctively hurrying to find the broken Rochester, Jane now moves with a new freedom. Her previous journeys have been routed by her elders (Gateshead-hall to Lowood), dictated by the need to escape from a deadening, enclosed world (Lowood to Thornfield), or prompted by conscience, like Christian's (Thornfield to Moor House). Now she challenges the Bible's and the *Progress*'s distinction between the narrow and the broad way, unquestioningly accepted by Brocklehurst and Rivers, and finds in retracing her steps to Thornfield that the Moor House phase, rather than her time at Thornfield, has been a detour, albeit an instructive one.[2] Her true path lies towards Ferndean. In order to find this path, Jane interprets a cry which only she can hear, rather than reading outward and visible signs as she did earlier in her life.

Reunited with her damaged Samson, Jane hears his account of his own Bunyanesque struggle: 'Divine justice pursued its course; disasters came thick on me: I was forced to pass through the valley of the shadow of death. *His* chastisements are mighty; and one smote me which has humbled me for ever' (37). In the final chapter (38: 'Conclusion'), Jane describes her marriage in terms of the union between the biblical Adam and Eve: 'No woman was ever nearer to her mate than I am: ever more absolutely bone of his bone, and flesh of his flesh' (cf. Genesis 2.23). Both partners have suffered before achieving this harmony. Rochester has undergone a period of Christian purgation and has been made physically unattractive. Jane has been humiliated, both on the moors and under St John's scrutiny, but has rejected fanatical Christian zeal for a moderate position dictated by Nature's promptings. This moderation is in the spirit of the Christian God who allows Rochester sufficient vision to see his new-born son: 'On that occasion, he again, with a full heart, acknowledged that God had tempered judgment with mercy.'

Jane Eyre ends with an outline of the Rivers' lives until the time of writing. Like Jane herself, Diana and Mary are happily married. St John has become an 'indefatigable pioneer' in India, a 'Greatheart, who guards his pilgrim-convoy from the on-slaught of Apollyon'. Jane knows that he will soon die, and that 'no fear of death will darken' his last hour. His crossing to the Celestial City will be an easy one. St John's work in India is the fruit of specialised reading: the Bible and 'crabbed oriental scrolls' in 'Hindostanee', the 'acquisition of which he thought necessary to his plans' (34). Jane's response to the cry, through which she is reunited with Rochester, is that of a comparatively wide-ranging reader, familiar with several modes of literature. On her journey from Gateshead-hall to Ferndean, no single reading, Gothic, biblical, Miltonic or Bunyanesque, has finally fixed her views. As a reader of literature, locations, and human behaviour, she has indeed proved to be a heroine 'in defiance of the accepted canon'.[3]

III

Brontë readers and critics have always acknowledged that the sisters' novels are extraordinary, difficult to place in relation to the mainstream of English fiction. Tom Winnifrith takes up an

extreme position on the question of their extraordinary qualities
when he states that the purpose of his recent study of *The
Brontës* is to show that they 'stand right outside any tradition,
and cannot be fitted into the history of the nineteenth-century
realistic novel'.⁴ He adds: 'Sometimes, especially in *Jane Eyre*
and *Wuthering Heights*, where realism seems to have been
subordinated to cosmic allegory, we seem to have moved far
away from the novel as a genre into the realm of romance.' I
would argue that romance is accommodated within a realistic
narrative, firmly, and partly through allusion, in *Jane Eyre*, and
precariously in *Wuthering Heights*, and that therefore these
novels cannot be said to stand *right* outside any tradition. The
unimaginative Nelly Dean and Lockwood act as controls in the
transmission of the extravagant tale of Heathcliff's devilish
doings, but they lose their way, taking the reader with them.
Jane Eyre, however, fulfils her reader-narrator contract, describing a recognisably real early nineteenth-century world which is
inhabited by recognisably nineteenth-century people. Most of
the allusions discussed above would have been as familiar to the
educated Victorian reader as the styles of architecture and
furniture described in each of the five houses in the novel. These
allusions indicate that *Jane Eyre* is as much a religious novel as a
romance and that it is to be read as a *spiritual* autobiography.
Jane's level-headed narration holds these different modes in
tension.

In subsequent chapters I will show that *Jane Eyre* shares
common concerns with other famous Victorian novels. For example, Dorothea's reading and the nature of her vision at the end
of *Middlemarch* are central themes in George Eliot's greatest
novel; and the way in which Jane is torn between two men looks
forward to Tess's problems with Angel and Alec in *Tess of the
d'Urbervilles*. Winnifrith himself writes: 'It is important to
remember that the Brontës were novelists of the 1840s, sharing
many of the preoccupations of their great contemporaries, even
though their isolation caused them to show their preoccupations
in a startlingly original way' (Winnifrith, p. 155). As we go on to
examine other Victorian novels it should also become clear that
Charlotte Brontë's use of allusion is similar to that of novelists in
the mainstream of realistic nineteenth-century fiction.

4

Dives versus Lazarus: *Mary Barton*

I

Those contemporary readers of *Wuthering Heights* who opened *Mary Barton: A Tale of Manchester Life* when it was published in two volumes a year later (1848) might have been excused for feeling that they were entering a world almost as 'rude and strange' as that of Ellis Bell's novel. Elizabeth Gaskell was acutely aware that most novel-readers lived south of the Trent. As a result, parts of *Mary Barton* read like a guide-book in which the author-narrator describes the alien world of the northern industrial worker to her middle-class readers in the south. Her husband William contributed explanatory foot-notes on dialect words and phrases, and, in the fifth (1854) edition, two lectures on the Lancashire Dialect, adding to the impression that Manchester Life was as foreign to most of the novel's readers as it had been to Elizabeth Gaskell herself when she first moved there in 1832, and was to be for Margaret Hale in *North and South* (1854–5). It would be wrong to assume, however, that the majority of middle-class readers were quite ignorant of the hardships suffered by the working-class in both the north and the south. Carlyle's attacks on both the Establishment and the Chartists in *Chartism* (1839) and *Past and Present* (1843) were widely read, making him the most influential and thought-provoking writer on the Condition of England Question of his time. Readers who lived through the Hungry Forties were bombarded with reformist essays in newspapers and journals, and could have read of working-class distress, often in northern industrial settings, in such novels as 'Charlotte Elizabeth's'

Helen Fleetwood (1839–40), Frances Trollope's *Michael Arm-
strong, the Factory Boy* (1840), and Disraeli's *Coningsby* (1844)
and *Sybil: or, The Two Nations* (1845). Poets of the 1830s had
opened up much of the ground which the better social-problem
novelists, such as Elizabeth Gaskell and Charles Kingsley,
developed in subsequent decades: Caroline Bowles in her *Tales
of the Factories* (1833) and Caroline Norton in *A Voice from the
Factories* (1836), for example. The early chapters of *Mary
Barton*, however, present the first truly *intimate* picture of
working-class life in the industrial north, focusing on the homes
of working people rather than the satanic mills and unventilated
work-rooms around which earlier reformist writers dragged
their unwilling readers.

The novel made a strong impression in literary circles and
among the wider reading public, appearing in the year of European revolutions. The Chartists, who came to public notice most
prominently in 1838–9 (the beginning of the period in which
Mary Barton is set) and 1848 (the year of its publication),
seemed to threaten to fulfil the prophecy of the young Engels in
The Condition of the Working-Class in England, published in
German in Leipzig in 1845: the only possible result of the
hardship and unrest among the working-class was revolution,
which would come soon. Published six months after the confron-
tation between the Establishment, personified in the Duke of
Wellington guarding the Houses of Parliament , and the Chartist
masses assembled south of the river in April 1848, *Mary Barton*
explores the motivations and frustrations of a Chartist and a
union man, John Barton, seen among his own people in their
urban environment. The houses and streets of Manchester are
shown to be inhabited by working men and women as various in
character and political stance as are their social 'superiors'. The
grey masses of the Industrial Revolution, alien and threatening,
are thus individualised in the early chapters of social realism in
the novel. In these moving chapters many middle-class readers
who lived in cities and towns where virtual class *apartheid* was in
force probably 'met' industrial workers for the first time.

Elizabeth Gaskell had to find ways in which to explain cus-
toms and habits of mind among the working-class which were
familiar to her (having long been involved in social work in
Manchester) but not to her readers. One way was to describe the
home life of her working-class characters in minute detail. Thus

middle-class readers were able to compare Mrs Barton's furniture with their own, and could contrast the appalling conditions in which the Davenports lived with those of their own well-fed servants. Another way was to explore contrasts between classes within the novel. Elizabeth Gaskell examines two kinds of cultural clash between Dives and Lazarus, rich and poor in *Mary Barton*. In the first half of the novel she shows how the classes collide head-on in the central love triangle and in the murder plot, and she relates this clash to the contrast between middle-class and working-class cultures. In the second half she shows that the conflict between John Barton and Mr Carson senior is based upon different misreadings of the Bible. Both the social realism of the first half and the parable of the second are underpinned with allusions.

II

Balladry is the special province of the female working-class characters in *Mary Barton*, who compare themselves to the familiar victim figures of the traditional ballad. Mary Barton's true cultural roots are suggested through references to the Carpenter's Wife (4), Donald's lover of 'The Siller Crown' (8) and Barbara Allen (12). All are girls of humble origin who are tempted by wealth or reject their working-class lovers. Attracted to the wealthy Harry Carson, Mary rejects her working-class suitor, Jem Wilson. She aspires to the social station of a lady and Carson's sisters' life-style, which is economically sketched in chapter 18. The older sisters are sleepy after a dancing-party the night before and listlessly turn the pages of Emerson's essays and a 'parcel of new songs', while the youngest copies manuscript music. The activities of these young ladies contrast strongly with those of the female working-class characters who have dominated the reader's attention throughout the first half of the novel.

This kind of contrast between classes is particularly marked in the chapters of *Mary Barton* in which Mary rejects Jem Wilson, later regretting her decision, and also dismisses the wealthy Carson. Like Mary, Wilson is associated with literature which has a special resonance for members of his class, in his case the poetry of Burns. The first of the two mottoes which head chapter

11 is from the poem 'Mary Morison':

> 'O Mary, canst thou wreck his peace,
> Wha for thy sake wad gladly die?
> Or canst thou break that heart of his,
> Whase only fault is loving thee?'
>
> BURNS

This motto is an excellent choice for the chapter in which Wilson's offer of marriage is spurned. First, the girl's name fits the context in the novel; secondly, the reader who knows the poem will recognise in Wilson the characteristic honesty and earnestness of Burns's disappointed lover, and thus be encouraged to compare him favourably with Carson; thirdly, the motto establishes the association between Wilson and Burns's poetry which is developed later in the novel. In chapter 15, Wilson confronts Carson in the street, wrongly believing that Mary is still seeing her 'gentleman' admirer: Carson 'seemed to the poor smith so elegant, so well appointed, that he felt the superiority in externals, strangely and painfully, for an instant. Then something uprose within him, and told him, that "a man's a man for a' that, for a' that, and twice as much as a' that." And he no longer felt troubled by the outward appearance of his rival.' Elizabeth Gaskell quotes a medley of refrains from Burns's poems here. The main adopted text, however, is the well-known song, 'For a' that and a' that', in which external appearances are said to be meaningless. Jem's uneasiness concerning what Burns calls the 'tinsel show' of fools and knaves is dispelled by his self-respect as a man, 'for a' that'.

On the other hand, Harry Carson finds justification for his feeling of superiority in Shakespeare. He looks at Jem and recalls his own reflection in the mirror: 'It was impossible. No woman with eyes could choose the one when the other wooed. It was Hyperion to a Satyr. That quotation came aptly; he forgot "That a man's a man for a' that."' In Hamlet's first soliloquy he compares his dead father with Claudius: 'So excellent a king that was to this/Hyperion to a satyr' (*Hamlet*, I.2.139–40). The words 'No woman with eyes' are reminiscent of Hamlet's speech when he leads his mother to the portraits of old Hamlet and Claudius:

> Have you eyes?
> Could you on this fair mountain leave to feed,
> And batten on this moor? Ha! have you eyes?
>   (*Hamlet*, III.4.65–7)

By expressing their inner thoughts through contrasting allusions, Elizabeth Gaskell underlines the differences of education
and outlook which separate Wilson and Carson: the worthy
artisan who could read Burns after work and the wealthy young
master who would know his *Hamlet*.

   In the following chapter Harry Carson attacks the workmen
during the strike meeting so vehemently that their looks are
rendered 'more livid, their glaring eyes more fierce' (16). He also
draws a caricature of the ragged men as he sits listening to the
arguments, appending a 'hasty quotation from the fat knight's
well-known speech in Henry IV'. As it is passed around the
table, all the masters smile and nod their heads. One of the
delegates notices what is going on, retrieves the discarded
caricature after the meeting, and shows it to his friends. Angered
by the caricature and by the masters' attitude towards their case,
the men plot to assassinate young Carson. A quotation has
become a physical as well as an abstract element of the murder
plot. Carson probably chooses Falstaff's soliloquy from *I Henry
IV*, in which he describes his troops' clothes: 'There's not a shirt
and a half in all my company' (IV.2.42–3). One wonders how
many Victorian readers smiled and nodded their heads as they
recognised the allusion. Carson's knowledge of the play, his
choice of Falstaff's mocking words, the silver pencil with which
he draws, and his skill in drawing, are all complementary details
which help to build up a picture of this arrogant character whose
own actions lead to his death.

   The most important class-cultural allusion in *Mary Barton*
is also closely associated with the murder of Harry Carson,
but is first introduced earlier in the novel. When John Barton is
depressed after the abortive Chartist rally, Job Legh offers to
read him 'a bit on a poem as is written by a weaver like oursel. A
rare chap I'll be bound is he who could weave verse like this' (9).
(Typically, the vigour of Job's response to the poem, like that of
his grand-daughter Margaret to ballads and oratorios, compares
favourably with the jumped-up Carsons' half-hearted attempts
to cultivate their sensibilities.) He then settles down to read:

So adjusting his spectacles on nose, cocking his chin, crossing his legs, and coughing to clear his voice, he read aloud a little poem of Samuel Bamford's* he had picked up somewhere.

* The fine-spirited author of 'Passages in the Life of a Radical' – a man who illustrates his order, and shows what nobility may be in a cottage.

Samuel Bamford (1788–1872) was a famous weaver-poet who lived near Manchester. Elizabeth Gaskell knew him and received a congratulatory letter from him when *Mary Barton* was published. He was probably one of William Gaskell's 'Poets of Humble Life', included in the lectures he gave to poor weavers in 1838.[1] The poem which Job reads, 'God Help the Poor', was included in James Wheeler's *Manchester Poetry* (1838), along with five other Bamford poems and William Gaskell's own 'Death and Sleep' and 'Come and Pray'. Elizabeth Gaskell's foot-note in *Mary Barton* suggests that she was keen to point out that the poem about to be quoted was written by a worthy member of the working-class. Like Margaret Jennings's rendition of 'The Oldham Weaver' (4), the quotation and the narrator's comments on Bamford educated the middle-class reader in the ways of the working-class. The first stanza of the poem sets the tone for the whole:

> God help the poor, who, on this wintry morn,
>   Come forth from alleys dim and courts obscure.
> God help yon poor pale girl, who droops forlorn,
>   And meekly her affliction doth endure;
> God help her, outcast lamb; she trembling stands,
> All wan her lips, and frozen red her hands;
> Her sunken eyes are modestly downcast,
> Her night-black hair streams on the fitful blast;
> Her bosom, passing fair, is half revealed,
> And oh! so cold, the snow lies there congealed;
> Her feet benumbed, her shoes all rent and worn,
> God help thee, outcast lamb, who standst forlorn!
>   God help the poor!

When the reading is over, John Barton asks Job if he can have a copy of the poem: 'So Mary took the paper. And the next day, on a blank half-sheet of a valentine she had once suspected to come from Jem Wilson—she copied Bamford's beautiful little poem.' A

piece of this valentine is later used by Barton as wadding in the
murder weapon (a gun borrowed from Jem Wilson), and a scrap
of the paper is discovered at the scene of the crime by Esther, the
prostitute (21). She gives it to Mary, who destroys it, now
realising that her father murdered Carson. The police arrest
Wilson and bring him to trial, knowing that he has recently had
an angry exchange with Carson, his rival lover. They pursue the
line of reasoning which, for the reader, is symbolically represented by the valentine greeting on the card. The motive of the
actual murderer (John Barton) is symbolically represented by
the Bamford poem written on the 'blank half-sheet' of the card.
Barton avenges the poor.

The shooting of Carson with a gun which is symbolically as
well as explosively charged is contrived and over-elaborate,
particularly as the piece of valentine card inscribed with Bamford's poem is Barton's answer to that other piece of paper on
which Carson scribbled the quotation from *Henry IV*, and which
happened to fall into the hands of the strikers! Bamford's poem,
however, is a justified indictment of the smug indifference shown
by the masters towards the plight of their starving workers, and
the contrast between the Bamford and Shakespeare allusions
complements that between the references to ballads and Emerson, and to Burns and Shakespeare. Although familiar to the
middle-class reader, the Burns and the ballads have a special
potency for the proud working-class characters who suffer
without resorting to revenge.

III

In her portrayal of the conflict between the real murderer, John
Barton, and Mr Carson senior, Elizabeth Gaskell uses allusion in
a different way, showing that worker and master draw on the
same source, the Bible, in defence of their views and actions, but
that they interpret the Bible in ways which reflect the prejudices
of their classes.

When masters and hands are driven to thoughts of violence
and revenge in *Mary Barton* they are judged in relation to New
Testament teaching. A steady flow of biblical allusions serves as
a kind of continuo in the novel. Elizabeth Gaskell as narrator,

and her worthiest and generally most conservative working-
class characters, of whom most of her readers would have
approved, quote innumerable texts of forgiveness and lay special
emphasis on Christ's teaching on the poor and the meek in the
Sermon on the Mount. Many of these allusions could be used to
illustrate the broad principles upon which Unitarian ethics were
based in the mid-nineteenth century. The history of English
Unitarianism is notoriously complex, largely because each religious community, centred on a chapel, prided itself on its
individuality of interpretation of Unitarian principles. Although
it is virtually impossible to define exactly what those principles
were, or to determine precisely how William and Elizabeth
Gaskell stood in relation to their fellow Unitarians, it is safe to
say that four basic themes (excluding the important anti-
Trinitarian dogma) run through the sermons and essays of both
conservative and liberal wings of the Unitarian movement.[2]
First, Unitarians believe that God is merciful in nature. Secondly, no sinner is damned to everlasting punishment after death.
Thirdly, the New Testament offers men and women a system of
ethics on which everyday morality should be based. Fourthly,
charitable conduct is the outward mark of the true Christian.
William Ellery Channing, the leading American Unitarian of his
day, wrote in a sermon of 1819: 'Our religion, we believe, lies
chiefly in the New Testament.'[3] Edgar Wright has suggested
that

> Mrs Gaskell's world is not merely a Christian one, it is a
> selectively New Testament one, discarding the Hebraic ele-
> ment which gave religion much of its authority in the Victorian
> period. Furthermore, a religion of love is necessarily a religion
> that must rely heavily on example and influence; the emphasis
> is . . . thrown on conduct. Such a point of view will tend
> naturally to themes and plots involving reconciliation, which
> is what we find in her novels.[4]

In their mutual distrust and, later, hatred, John Barton and Mr
Carson senior distort or reject the teaching of the New Testament
on which Unitarianism was based.

On his death-bed, John Barton describes the series of spiritual
and moral crises which led to his murdering Harry Carson, and
speaks of his former belief in the Bible and subsequent disillu-

sionment. Although the death of his son Tom weakened his faith and intensified his hatred of the masters, he still tried to love all men, including the masters:

> 'I was tore in two oftentimes, between my sorrow for poor suffering folk, and my trying to love them as caused their sufferings (to my mind). . . . At last I gave it up in despair, trying to make folks' actions square wi' th' Bible; and I thought I'd no longer labour at following th' Bible mysel. I've said all this afore, may be. But from that time I've dropped down, down–down'. (35)

Barton's fall can be traced from the earliest chapters of the novel. On their walk in Green Heys Fields he discusses the absent Esther with George Wilson (1). A long rhetorical speech of Barton's has a function in the novel similar to that of a text heading a sermon, indicating themes which are to be developed later. His biblical allusions in the speech betray the biases of his class. For example, he would hate to see Mary becoming like a lady: 'I'd rather see her earning her bread by the sweat of her brow, as the Bible tells her she should do, ay, though she never got butter to her bread, then be like a do-nothing lady' (cf. Genesis 3.19). His attack on the rich is based on Christ's description of the Last Judgment (Matthew 25.32–6):

> 'If I am sick do they come and nurse me? If my child lies dying (as poor Tom lay, with his white wan lips quivering, for want of better food than I could give him), does the rich man bring the wine or broth that might save his life? If I am out of work for weeks in the bad times, and winter comes, with black frost, and keen east wind, and there is no coal for the grate, and no clothes for the bed, and the thin bones are seen through the ragged clothes, does the rich man share his plenty with me, as he ought to do, if his religion wasn't a humbug?. . . No, I tell you, it's the poor, and the poor only, as does such things for the poor.'

Barton develops his argument when he and George Wilson discuss their masters in the Davenports' cellar, asking his friend: 'How comes it they're rich, and we're poor? I'd like to know that. Han they done as they'd be done by for us?' (6).

Barton's use of biblical texts as a scourge with which to beat the masters is reminiscent of earlier radical writings. For example, the proverbial form of Christ's words in the Sermon on the Mount (Matthew 7.12) is quoted by Tom Paine in *The Rights of Man*, Part I (1791): 'The duty of man is not a wilderness of turnpike gates, through which he is to pass by tickets from one to the other. It is plain and simple, and consists but of two points. His duty to God, which every man must feel; and with respect to his neighbour, to do as he would be done by.'[5] Like John Barton, Paine applies Christ's words to a society in which the rich appear not to have heard them.

Barton's third biblical allusion in the speech in chapter 1 betrays his bitterness: '"We pile up their fortunes with the sweat of our brows, and yet we are to live as separate as if we were in two worlds; ay, as separate as Dives and Lazarus, with a great gulf betwixt us: but I know who was best off then," and he wound up his speech with a low chuckle that had no mirth in it.' Barton's application of biblical texts is ominously restricted to the condemnation of the rich. In his quotation from the parable of Dives and Lazarus he shows that he has a detailed knowledge of the passage in Luke's gospel. The rich man ('Dives' in the Vulgate) asks Abraham to send Lazarus to cool his tongue with water, for while he is 'tormented' in hell, Lazarus rests in the bosom of Abraham: 'But Abraham said, Son, remember that thou in thy lifetime receivedst thy good things, and likewise Lazarus evil things: but now he is comforted, and thou are tormented./And beside all this, between us and you there is a great gulf fixed: so that they which would pass from hence to you cannot; neither can they pass to us, that would come from thence' (Luke 16.25–6). It has rightly been suggested that, at the end of Barton's speech, 'our Lord's intention in the parable is perverted by this suggestion of delight in prospective revenge'.[6]

This parable seems to nag at Barton as he grows increasingly embittered. When he returns from London he says of the metropolis: 'Ay, London's a fine place . . . and finer folk live in it than I ever thought on, or ever heerd tell on except in th' story-books. They are having their good things now, that afterwards they may be tormented' (9). Elizabeth Gaskell ensures that the reader does not miss the otherwise unmarked quotation by adding this gloss: 'Still at the old parable of Dives and Lazarus! Does it haunt the minds of the rich as it does those of the poor?' Before the fatal strike meeting with the masters, several pages are devoted to a detailed description of Barton's state of mind: 'John Barton's overpowering thought, which was to work out his fate on earth, was rich and poor; *why are they so separate*, so distinct, when God has made them all? It is not His will that their interests are so far apart. Whose doing is it?' (15; my emphasis). The parable still dominates his thoughts. Not willing to wait for some kind of heavenly reward, he takes his own revenge. After his death, Job Legh discusses his life with Mr Carson and tries to explain his dilemma: 'You see he were sadly put about to make great riches and great poverty square with Christ's Gospel. . . . It seemed hard to him that a heap of gold should part him and his brother so far asunder' (37). While recognising Barton's misinterpretation of the parable, the mid-dle-class Victorian reader is to remember that the masters' Dives-like attitude towards their workers was the main cause of his bitterness and his subsequent perversion of Christ's message.

Mr Carson's interpretation of the Bible is as distorted as Barton's. His first reaction to the death of his son is intense: 'My son! my son! . . . you shall be avenged, my poor murdered boy' (18). He unconsciously echoes David's lament after the death of Absalom: 'O my son Absalom, my son, my son Absalom! would God I had died for thee, O Absalom, my son, my son!' (II Samuel 18.33). (Later in the novel Harry Carson is explicitly described as his father's 'darling, his Absalom' (32).) But Carson's initial wave of grief immediately drives him to find his son's murderer and to see him hanged. When Jem Wilson is arrested, Mary is anxious to save him from 'the doom awaiting the shedder of blood' of Ezekiel (22). A 'shedder of blood' shall 'surely die; his blood shall be upon him' (Ezekiel 18.10, 13). While Mary Barton is delirious, after Jem's trial, she fears her father as a 'blood-shedder' (33). She recovers, however, and decides to try to bear everything for her father's sake, pitifully, as one who knows of 'some awful curse awaiting the blood-shedder' (34). Elizabeth Gaskell adds: 'All along she had felt it difficult (as I may have said before) to reconcile the two ideas, of her father and a blood-shedder.' Hanging, the doom awaiting the shedder of blood, will not be necessary. Barton's own conscience kills him. When Carson visits Barton and hears his confession he can see that he is dying and yet still wants him to be hanged: '"Oh, sir!" said Mary, springing forward, and catching hold of Mr Carson's arm, "my father is dying. Look at him, sir. If you want Death for Death, you have it. Don't take him away from me these last hours"' (35). Mary's words indicate that Carson's ethical code is based on the famous text in Exodus (21.23–5). Christ's teaching on these verses, in the Sermon on the Mount, is equally famous: 'Ye have heard that it hath been said, An eye for an eye, and a tooth for a tooth:/But I say unto you, That ye resist not evil: but whosoever shall smite thee on thy right cheek, turn to him the other also' (Matthew 5.38–9). Mary's words to Carson suggest that he is unwittingly ignoring Christ's crucial amendment of the Law.

Whereas Barton is the 'shedder of blood', Carson is the 'avenger'. At the trial he is described as 'the avenger of blood' (32), and later, beside Barton's death-bed, as 'the Avenger, the sure Avenger' (35). The role of the avenger is described in the Old Testament: 'But if any man hate his neighbour, and lie in wait for him, and rise up against him, and smite him mortally that he die, and fleeth into one of these cities [of refuge]:/Then the elders of his city shall send and fetch him thence, and deliver him into the hand of the avenger of blood, that he may die' (Deuteronomy 19.11–12). Barton hates his neighbour, lies in wait for him, rises up against him, and smites him mortally that he dies. He is then delivered into the hand of the avenger of blood, Mr Carson. When the latter is about to leave Barton's house he breaks down, thinking of his dead son. He 'cries aloud' for the 'comfort' given to the Children of Israel, of which Margaret Jennings sang earlier (Isaiah 40.1), but refuses to forgive Barton's 'trespasses', adding, 'Let my trespasses be unforgiven, so that I may have vengeance for my son's murder' (Matthew 6.14–15). Carson openly rejects the Christian principle of forgiveness.

Up to this point in the plot, the contrasts between Barton's and Carson's readings of the Bible, and the use of biblical allusion to illustrate those contrasts, have been handled, if not with great subtlety, at least with tact. The scene which follows is disastrously contrived. On his way home Carson sees a little girl knocked over in the street by an errand-boy. Her nurse is about to find a policeman but is stopped by the bleeding, tearful girl: '"Please, dear nurse, I'm not much hurt; it was very silly to cry, you know. He did not mean to do it. *He did not know what he was doing*, did you, little boy? Nurse won't call a policeman, so don't be frightened.'' And she put up her little mouth to be kissed by her injurer, just as she had been taught to do at home to "make peace"' (35). This fortuitous encounter, on which Carson's conversion turns, is reminiscent of maudlin scenes in the improving tracts for the young which educated Victorian mothers bought for their daughters. The words which Elizabeth Gaskell emphasises remind Carson of something: 'He had some association with those words; he had heard, or read of that plea somewhere before. Where was it?. . .Could it be–?' His questions are reminiscent of Scrooge's in stave IV of *A Christmas Carol* (1843). The Ghost of Christmas Yet to Come shows Scrooge the Cratchit family after the supposed death of Tiny Tim. Peter Cratchit is reading aloud: '"And He took a child, and set him in the midst of them." Where had Scrooge heard those words? He had not dreamed them. The boy must have read them out, as he and the Spirit crossed the threshold. Why did he not go on?' Both Dickens and Elizabeth Gaskell implicitly invite their readers to supply the answers to these questions.

Mr Carson hurries home to read his Bible in a manner which suggests that Elizabeth Gaskell borrowed heavily from one of Caroline Bowles's wooden *Tales of the Factories* (1833): 'Pestilence–What May Be: A Dramatic Scene.'⁷ After reading one of the gospels straight through with eager attention, he comes to the end, 'the awful End'. The words of Christ on the cross haunt him: 'All night long, the Archangel combated with the Demon' (cf. Jude 1.9.). He returns to Barton's house early in the morning and finds that he is dying. Mary asks him to pray for them:

No other words would suggest themselves than some of those he had read only a few hours before–
'God be merciful to us sinners–Forgive us our
trespasses as we forgive them that trespass against us.'
And when the words were said, John Barton lay a corpse
in Mr Carson's arms.
So ended the tragedy of a poor man's life.

The key verses on which Carson's mind works in chapter 35 are all texts of forgiveness: 'Father, forgive them; for they know not what they do' (Luke 23.34); 'Forgive us our trespasses, as we forgive them that trespass against us' (Matthew 6.12, 14–15; Book of Common Prayer version); and the words of the publican in the parable, 'God be merciful to me a sinner' (Luke 18.13). In the chapter of Barton's death, Carson's conversion dominates the reader's attention. (It is important to note that Barton is left in a critical condition while Carson is described returning home.) Elizabeth Gaskell uses his conversion from Old Testament to New Testament ethics to illustrate how, in her opinion, Practical Christianity (a favourite Unitarian phrase) can help to end the cycle of revenge set in motion by bitterness and hatred between classes. The set pieces of the chapter (the scene in the street, Carson's night of soul-searching and the death-bed scene) are underpinned with crucial biblical allusions which the reader must recognise in order to understand the full significance of Carson's change of heart.

IV

It was the Dickens of the Christmas Books who responded favourably to *Mary Barton* and pleaded for stories for *Household Words* from its author. (Dickens himself attended Little Portland Street Unitarian chapel for over a year in his early thirties, where he probably found the emphasis on charity and forgiveness compatible with his own faith in 'the teaching of the New Testament in its broad spirit'.[8]) The modern reader has to make the same historical allowances when reading the reconciliation scenes in *Mary Barton* that he does when reading *A Christmas Carol*. Victorian fictional versions of New Testament parables[9] often seem highly sugared to a reader living in a cynical age, whereas Victorian readers, more familiar with their own novelists' conventions and closer to the potent religious sources on which many of those conventions were based, bought and read Dickens's Christmas Books avidly, and must have found the reconciliation between John Barton and Mr Carson more acceptable than most modern readers do. We should not make too many historical allowances, however, when analysing the obvious faults in *Mary Barton*, some of which are attributable to, or at least highlighted by Elizabeth Gaskell's use of allusion in the novel.

Many of the faults in this first novel seem to have resulted from what one might call 'over-writing'. Elizabeth Gaskell drew on years of observation and untapped creative talent when she wrote the novel in her late thirties, and tried to pack too much into the work. Much of the melodramatic plotting in the novel, such as the mill fire (5) and the pursuit of Will Wilson (22–32), is redundant. Similarly, there are too many deaths. These weaknesses are counterbalanced, however, by the sheer energy of the narrative and the emotional intensity of the portrayal of hardship and despair among the working people of Manchester. The strengths and weaknesses of *Mary Barton* often share a common source. The redundancy of many of the biblical texts of forgiveness which permeate the novel should be set against the real power of John Barton's biblical rhetoric and of the shift from Old Testament to New Testament ethics in the final chapters of the novel. Adverse modern criticism of *Mary Barton* has tended to focus on the change in texture, almost, some would argue, in mode, which takes place after the murder (18), that is, in the second of the two volumes of the first edition. Let us briefly consider modern criticism of the murder plot in relation to my discussion of biblical allusion above.

Raymond Williams writes: 'As compared with the carefully representative character of the early chapters, the murder itself is exceptional.'[10] The murder is certainly exceptional within the context of the novel, but is prepared for from the early chapters, where Barton's verbal attacks on the masters are ferocious. Elizabeth Gaskell portrays John Barton gradually isolating himself after the death of his wife (in chapter 3) and eventually becoming exceptionally antagonistic towards the masters. He is at first one of a few radicals–'among these few was John Barton' (3), 'one of them was John Barton' (8), 'among them was John Barton' (15)–being both a Chartist delegate and a representative of the workmen in the Union. Eventually he becomes the one man to represent them all, having drawn the lot to murder Harry Carson. After the murder, the submerged parables of the first half of the novel, indicated through Barton's biblical allusions, surface when the particular and exceptional (Barton murders Harry Carson but is later reconciled with his father) illustrates the general and unexceptional (the workers hate the masters but will later recognise changes of attitude among them).

Williams describes the Barton-Carson reconciliation and the emigration of the surviving working-class characters to Canada as a 'kind of writing-off' (Williams, p. 102). Stephen Gill makes a similar point in the introduction to his edition of the novel: 'One feels the second part to be in quite a different and a lesser genre from the first. It seems as if a complex re-creation of events, scenes and problems concerning the real circumstances of the 1840s has given way to a more simple fable which ends in a moral tableau.'[11] Gill's statement that the second part is in 'quite a different and a *lesser* genre from the first' is related to his sensitive appreciation of the dense realism which makes the opening chapters of the novel one of the best portrayals of working-class life in nineteenth-century fiction. The readers for whom the novel was written probably read it differently. I have already shown that the parabolic incidents in the second half of the novel are associated with potent religious analogues; potent, that is, to the reader who follows the strands of biblical allusion throughout the novel. Gill does not point out that the constituent elements of the 'fable' are embedded in the first part of *Mary Barton*, submerged under the realistic surface of incident and dialogue in which the reader is primarily engaged. For example, Barton's speeches in Green Heys Fields (1) and in the Davenports' cellar (6), rich with biblical allusions which define his class consciousness, determine the kind of analogical interpretation which is expected of the reader: Barton as an avenging Lazarus, the poor and the rich as the sheep and the goats, and the rich as a group defying Christ's command to 'Do as you would be done by'. In 1848, the year of European revolutions and the death of Chartism in England, the contemporary reader of *Mary Barton* was far more likely than most modern critics to recognise and appreciate the associative power of these allusions.[12] One tends, however, to accept a conventional device such as the conversion of a character or a reconciliation scene in a Victorian novel only if characterisation and plot justify and support that device. When the plot creaks, as it does in chapter 35 of *Mary Barton*, a conventional device becomes mere contrivance. Elizabeth Gaskell made the mistake of relying upon her parabolic structure to suggest a viable way out for her characters and the real inhabitants of Manchester. (Williams and Gill are justified in their criticisms to this extent.) Similarly, the shift from the first half of the novel, in which the love-plot and the murder-plot are subordinated to the social themes, to the reverse position in the second half, pivoting on the double-sided valentine card, satisfies the needs of the novelist structuring her narrative, but leaves problems unsolved in its over-neatness. Nevertheless, Elizabeth Gaskell does succeed in accommodating parable within her social realism through allusion, bringing the Condition of England Question home to her readers as a crucial test case, Dives versus Lazarus, to which Christian ethics should be applied.

5

Apocalypse in a Mechanical Age: *Hard Times*

I

Dickens was one of several leading literary figures of the day who greatly admired *Mary Barton* and who met its author when she was lionised in London in 1849. Elizabeth Gaskell accepted Dickens's invitation to contribute to his newly established weekly, *Household Words*, the following year and went on to publish *Cranford, North and South* and numerous short stories in its pages. Less obviously than in this collaboration, harmonious before the publication of *North and South* in 1854–5, the novelists' mutual respect can be gauged by the influence of Dickens's portrayal of Little Em'ly and Steerforth in *David Copperfield* (1849–50) on Gaskell's handling of her heroine's relationship with Henry Bellingham in *Ruth* (1853), and the debt which Dickens owed to Gaskell in his turn in *Hard Times* (1854), where Harthouse's 'going in for' politics, Tom Gradgrind's crime, and other elements of the plot are variations on themes from *Ruth*. Similarities between *Mary Barton* and *Hard Times* are more suggestive of common concerns and shared values than of inter-textual influence. Both novels focus on victims of industrialisation and of what Carlyle saw as the accompanying mechanisation of every aspect of human activity, from labour and trade to education and worship ('Signs of the Times'). Both end with a member of the older generation undergoing a drastic change of heart and mind after a traumatic experience involving his child or children, a favourite motif of both Dickens and Gaskell, also used in *Dombey and Son* and *Ruth* among other novels. The polemics of both novels are based on New Testament ethics. In other respects, however, the two novels could hardly be more different. Dickens's language, symbolism and characterisation constantly remind the reader that the novel is a fanciful artifice, and that his descriptions of Coketown are prose poems. Whereas *Hard Times* can be compared to a grotesque, highly coloured oil painting, *Mary Barton* is suggestive of early photography in the realism of its early chapters, where characters are portrayed against the sharply focused background of a specific Victorian industrial town. The contrast between the endings of the two novels illustrates another fundamental difference. Elizabeth Gaskell adopts a familiar nineteenth-century novelistic convention when she ends *Mary Barton* with a glimpse of the future for her characters: 'I see a long low wooden house, with room enough and to spare' (38). Mary and Jem Wilson live in Canada with their little son and Wilson's mother. The security of family life in a land of opportunities seems assured. Margaret Jennings's sight has been restored and she is to join the Wilsons in Canada, accompanied by her new husband, Will, and old Job Legh. The weak last line of the novel is Mary's: '"Dear Job Legh!" said Mary, softly and seriously.' In the last chapter of *Hard Times*, 'Final', Dickens also looks forward in time but emphasises the fact that the characters 'garner' the harvest they have 'sown' and 'reaped' in their earthly lives. Having in effect judged his characters, ending with Sissy, who is to become a happy and much loved mother, he turns to his reader in the last paragraph of the novel: 'Dear reader! It rests with you and me, whether, in our two fields of action, similar things shall be or not. Let them be! We shall sit with lighter bosoms on the hearth, to see the ashes of our fires turn grey and cold' (III.9). Dickens ends with his own and his reader's endings. In *Hard Times*, written in Dickens's most prophetic style, images of fire and ashes suggest that death is ever present in the hell of Coketown.[1] The novel ends with the formerly 'implied' reader overtly addressed and thus included in Dickens's judgment of modern 'civilisation'.[2] Like Louisa Gradgrind, who is obsessed with fire and ashes, the reader comes to contemplate the Four Last Things of eschatology: death, judgment, heaven and hell.

With one notable exception, modern critics have paid little attention to the numerous biblical allusions in *Hard Times* which its contemporary readers would not have missed.[3] These allusions have an important function in relation to Dickens's symbolism in a work which, unlike *Mary Barton*, is more than a 'social-problem novel'. The allusions to biblical texts which touch on the theme of the Four Last Things are particularly important. As Geoffrey Rowell has shown in his study of *Hell and the Victorians* (1974), eschatology was 'not a new subject of controversy in the nineteenth century, but there is little doubt that it was discussed more publicly, and perhaps with more vehemence, than in any previous age'.[4] Rowell quotes splendid examples of sermons and meditations in which the horrors of the grave and the terrors of eternal damnation were luridly described by Victorian preachers. H. P. Liddon, one of Pusey's disciples, compiled a volume of private meditations entitled *The End of Life* (1858) which included seven meditations on death. The irreversible onset of physical decay after death is graphically described in meditation 32:

[Dying] is to hand over this body in which I have so long thought, loved, walked, slept, prayed, and which I have so often indulged – to humiliations, which must seem painful and degrading, to an utter solitude where I shall see nothing, not even the labours of the worms which will have taken possession of my entire person, where I shall become the food of creatures from which I should have shrunk with loathing, and shall gradually lose form and feature and subside into a mess of corrupt infection – which in time will resolve itself into my native dust. (Rowell, p. 111)

Victorians developed strong stomachs for this kind of thing, as they were forced to consider the physical reality of the degeneration of the body when earth is committed to earth, ashes to ashes, and dust to dust, more often than are most of their descendants today. Pusey himself, never a noted 'hell-fire' preacher, delivered a sermon in 1856 which, years later, he came to see was a rather extreme treatment of the 'terrors of the Lord':

This, then, is the first outward suffering of the damned, that they are purged, steeped in a lake of fire. . . . You know the fierce, intense, burning, heat of a furnace, how it consumes in a moment anything cast into it. Its misery to the damned shall be that they feel it, but cannot be consumed by it. The fire shall pierce them, penetrate them: it shall be, Scripture says, like a molten 'lake of fire', rolling, tossing, immersing, but not destroying. (Rowell, p. 108)

ay sermons, heard and read, and regular Bible reading
antly reminded the mid-Victorians that the grave and
possibly hell itself yawned beneath their feet. For Dickens's
contemporaries the immanence of death, judgment, heaven and
hell was a central received idea, frequently conveyed through
terrifying visual images of the grave and hell fire.

Apart from Blake, Dickens's most important precursor who
applied biblical prophecy to industrial society, and invoked the
Four Last Things in his apocalyptic writings on the state of the
nation, was Carlyle. Dickens does more than pay homage to
Carlyle as a mentor in the novel which is inscribed to him. He
adapts many of his ideas on the Condition of England Question
and some of his most powerful images and metaphors, mainly
from 'Signs of the Times' (1829), *Sartor Resartus* (1833–4) and
Chartism (1839).[5] The most interesting and least noticed influence which Carlyle had on *Hard Times* is partly a matter of tone
and partly of content: Dickens is *prophetic* in a way which
strongly echoes Carlyle, whose thundering attacks on the
Mechanical Age were familiar to many of the novelist's readers.
Whereas Carlyle's essays have certain novelistic features,
such as illustrative fictional vignettes and fictional narrators,
Dickens's novel sometimes reads like a propagandist tract or
essay. Carlyle's essays and *Hard Times* draw on apocalyptic
passages from the Bible in their portrayals of the suppression of
the 'dynamical' by the 'mechanical' ('Signs of the Times'), and
in their attacks on Utilitarianism. For Gradgrind, as for Carlyle's contemporary readers, the Writing was on the Wall.
Dickens exploits the possibilities of eschatological allusion and
symbolism in his prophetic authorial commentary in a typically
imaginative way, closely linking this commentary to his portrayal of Coketown and the surrounding countryside (the hell
without) and his exploration of some of his central characters'
inner lives (the hell within).

II

Like Gradgrind's Stone Lodge (I.3) and Bounderby's 'brazen
plate' and 'brazen' handle on his door (I.11), Coketown itself is
an extension of its masters: 'Coketown, to which Messrs Bounderby and Gradgrind now walked, was a triumph of fact' (I.5)

The novel's book titles, 'Sowing', 'Reaping' and 'Garnering', and its opening paragraph, in which Gradgrind tells M'Choak-cumchild to 'plant' nothing but facts in the minds of the school children, imply that whatsoever Gradgrind 'soweth, that shall he also reap' (Galatians 6.7; cf. Job 4.8). Of course, in the early stages of 'Sowing', Gradgrind is well pleased with his educational enterprise. He walks homeward from the school 'in a state of considerable satisfaction' after setting M'Choakcumchild to work (I.3). The later undermining of Gradgrindery, particularly as applied to education and exemplified in the failure of the method by which Tom and Louisa Gradgrind are educated, fulfils the prophecy which is hinted at through symbolism and allusion early in the novel: Coketown, the product of logical thought and the 'triumph of fact', is a hell on earth when seen through the eyes of those who suffer in it rather than control its development. Commentators have agreed that Coketown is a 'perversion of nature'[6] or, more specifically, a 'perversion of cultivated nature'[7]. Its mills and machines are animated, its men and women mechanical. Carlyle's mechanical and dynamical are chaotically confused. In Coketown ''tis a' a muddle' in more senses than Stephen Blackpool's (I.11).

A perverted aspect of the town which must have disturbed many Victorian readers is the unconscious blasphemy against scriptural teaching implicit in Gradgrindery. Several allusions in *Hard Times* indicate the gap which separates the philosophy of Fact from New Testament teaching. The title of the first chapter, 'The One Thing Needful', makes the point straight away. Gradgrind's choice of 'nothing but Facts' compares unfavourably with Mary's choice of the one thing that is needful when she listens to Jesus's word at his feet (Luke 10.39–42). Dickens introduces the first of several apocalyptic allusions in the novel in his satirical attack on the government officer at the school: 'He had it in charge from high authority to bring about the great Public-office Millennium, when Commissioners should reign upon earth' (I.2). Placed in the chapter entitled 'Murdering the Innocents' and followed by descriptions of a hellish Coketown, this reference to a grotesque version of the Millennium is more than a passing dig at the commissioners. Later, again in his authorial commentary, Dickens implies that Fact has replaced God or heaven in Gradgrind's scheme of things, when he explains that the little Gradgrind children knew nothing of an

Ogre and adds, 'Fact forbid!' (I.3), predating Aldous Huxley's 'Our Ford' in *Brave New World* by eighty years. In Coketown, 'what you couldn't state in figures, or show to be purchaseable in the cheapest market and saleable in the dearest, was not, and never should be, world without end, Amen' (I.5). The laws of Fact have superseded the laws of God. Sissy Jupe blasphemes against the science of Political Economy when she states that its first principle is 'to do unto others as I would that they should do unto me' (I.9). Later in the novel, the ironic contrast is reversed: Gradgrind sits in his study 'proving something no doubt – probably, in the main, that the Good Samaritan was a Bad Economist' (II.12). Several characters in the novel (Slackbridge, Gradgrind, Bounderby, Harthouse and Mrs Sparsit) add to the chaos of perversions and inversions of received ethical lore by evangelising their own anti-gospels to whoever is within earshot in Coketown. Slackbridge is explicitly described as promulgating 'the gospel according to Slackbridge' (III.4). Throughout the novel, the gospel of the New Testament is the yardstick by which its modern usurpers are measured and found wanting.

Enveloped by the 'smoke and ashes' of Coketown (I.5), raised in the dryasdust world delimited by her father, and silenced by the insistent harangues of the people who control her life, Louisa Gradgrind turns in upon herself to contemplate the nature of her earthly existence and the future life. In her childhood she sits with her brother Tom in their study looking at the 'bright sparks' of the fire dropping on the hearth (I.8). Noticing that she constantly stares at the fire, Tom asks her what she sees there. At first she says that she does not 'see anything in it' but is wondering about herself and Tom 'grown up'. When her mother disapproves of her talking about 'wondering', she is more forthcoming: 'I was encouraged by nothing, mother, but by looking at the red sparks dropping out of the fire, and whitening and dying. It made me think, after all, how short my life would be, and how little I could hope to do in it.' Mrs Gradgrind is horrified to hear this metaphoric talk of 'sparks and ashes' from a girl who has benefited from lectures and experiments on 'combustion, and calcination, and calorification'.

Gradgrind himself scarcely notices how Louisa grows up, as she is 'so quiet and reserved, and so much given to watching the bright ashes at twilight' as they fall into the grate and become 'extinct' (I.14). Her thoughts on the ashes of her own fire, suggestive of the words from the Burial Service ('ashes to ashes'), have a larger significance when she turns her eyes to Coketown itself. Tom has just hinted that he wants her to make his way easy with Bounderby:

> She gave him an affectionate good-night, and went out with him to the door, whence the fires of Coketown could be seen, making the distance lurid. She stood there, looking steadfastly towards them, and listening to his departing steps. . . . It seemed as if, first in her own fire within the house, and then in the fiery haze without, she tried to discover what kind of woof Old Time, that greatest and longest-established Spinner of all, would weave from the threads he had already spun into a woman. But his factory is a secret place, his work is noiseless, and his Hands are mutes. (I.14).

Louisa sees no new heaven and new earth before her, as her father does, but a 'lurid' townscape in which 'the fiery haze' seems a bodying forth of her own inner hell. She does not wait long to discover what Old Time has in store for her. Her future is decided during the two interviews with her father in his 'Observatory' at Stone Lodge: the first immediately after her discussion with Tom about Bounderby and the second when she leaves Bounderby and escapes from Harthouse, returning to Stone Lodge.

Dickens's description of Gradgrind's activities in the Observatory strikes one of his 'key-notes': he 'had no need to cast an eye upon the teeming myriads of human beings around him, but could settle all their destinies on a slate, and wipe out all their tears with one dirty little bit of sponge' (I.15). The blasphemy of Gradgrind's playing God in his own little mechanical universe is registered by Dickens in the substitution of 'one dirty little bit of sponge' for the mysteries of the Revelation whereby God will wash the robes of earthly sufferers and 'wipe away all tears from their eyes' (Revelation 7.14,17). When Gradgrind discusses the possibility of marriage to Bounderby with Louisa, merely quoting marriage statistics in order to allay her fears about marrying an older man, other apocalyptic texts suggest how both he and his Utilitarian systems would be judged on the Last Day. In order to have seen that Louisa wanted to communicate her 'pent-up confidences', he 'must have overleaped at a bound the

artificial barriers he had for many years been erecting, between
himself and all those subtle essences of humanity which will
elude the utmost cunning of algebra until the last trumpet ever to
be sounded shall blow even algebra to wreck' (I.15). Dickens
follows this unambiguous if unmarked quotation from a later
chapter in Revelation (11) with a comment by Louisa which
emphasises the symbolic parallels between the fires of Coketown
and her inner self. She looks out at the town and says: 'There
seems to be nothing there but languid and monotonous smoke.
Yet when the night comes, Fire bursts out, father!' Listing the
dynamical aspects of life which she has never been allowed to
nurture, she closes her hand 'as if upon a solid object', and then
opens it 'as though she were releasing dust or ash'. Related
themes and motifs (including Louisa's thoughts on death and her
harping on ashes and fire), implied warnings that Gradgrindery
is to be judged and condemned, and hellish descriptions of
Coketown are inter-related in this interview between father and
daughter in which the seeds of disaster are sown. This penultimate chapter of 'Sowing' prophesies that Gradgrind has 'sown
the wind' and 'shall reap the whirlwind' (Hosea 8.7).

Dickens's apocalyptic allusions complement the less explicitly
referential symbolism of fire and ashes in 'Sowing'. Allusion and
symbolism also have complementary functions in 'Reaping' and
'Garnering', particularly where Dickens explores relations between his characters' inner lives and the landscape and
townscape in which they move. When she marries Bounderby,
Louisa lives with him in a large house about fifteen miles from
Coketown, accessible 'within a mile or two, by a railway striding
on many arches over a wild country, undermined by deserted
coal-shafts, and spotted at night by fires and black shapes of
stationary engines at pits' mouths' (II.7). To the railway traveller, this sinister land of pits and fires is a nether world. Dickens's
description of the no man's land between town and country, and
the later rescue of Stephen Blackpool from Old Hell Shaft, follow
in a tradition which has its roots in the early years of the
Industrial Revolution, with Blake, and develops through Carlyle's writings and John Martin's apocalyptic paintings. Francis
Klingender places a picture entitled 'Explosion and Fire at Shiff-
nal, near Wellington, Shropshire' (1821), in which fire and
smoke belch from a grimly satanic industrial site, alongside
Martin's famous painting of 'The Great Day of his Wrath',

exhibited in London and other cities in the early 1850s, in his study of *Art and the Industrial Revolution* (1947).[8] Most of Dickens's readers would have been familiar with such symbolic associations between industrialism and the stereotyped hell of bottomless pits and belching furnaces. When Louisa moves to the country with Bounderby, leaving the study fire at Stone Lodge and the fires which burst out at night in Coketown, she crosses a hellish landscape which is to figure in her escape from Harthouse, when she is pursued by Mrs Sparsit.

Dickens's satirical treatment of both Harthouse, the instigator of Louisa's crisis at the end of 'Reaping', and of Mrs Sparsit, its closest observer, is playfully ambiguous. Harthouse, a superfine representative of Carlyle's unworking aristocracy, has no 'earnest wickedness of purpose in him' and yet, like the villainous seducer of melodrama, has a devilish air which is as sinister as it is amusing:

> When the Devil goeth about like a roaring lion, he goeth about in a shape by which few but savages and hunters are attracted. But, when he is trimmed, smoothed, and varnished, according to the mode; when he is aweary of vice, and aweary of virtue, used up as to brimstone, and used up as to bliss; then, whether he take to the serving out of red tape, or to the kindling of red fire, he is the very Devil.
>
> (II.8; cf. I Peter 5.8; Revelation 21.8)

The wittily introduced 'brimstone' and 'red fire' have serious undertones when read in the context of Dickens's portrayal of Louisa, and of his description of Coketown and its environs, dotted with fires and black pits. Similarly, the phrase 'the very Devil' can be read in two ways: as the clubman's cliché for a dashed roguish fellow or as the actual Devil incarnate. Dickens's contemporary readers would have been familiar with the allusion to the devil going about as a roaring lion (I Peter) in other more straightforwardly moralistic contexts. For example, in Elizabeth Gaskell's *Ruth*, the heroine's old family friend, the labourer Thomas, tries to warn her that she is in danger of being tempted by the handsome Henry Bellingham, Harthouse's precursor:

> 'My dear, remember the devil goeth about as a roaring lion, seeking whom he may devour; remember that, Ruth.'

The words fell on her ear, but gave no definite idea. The utmost they suggested was the remembrance of the dread she felt as a child when this verse came into her mind, and how she used to imagine a lion's head with glaring eyes peering out of the bushes in a dark shady part of the wood. . . . She never imagined that the grim warning related to the handsome young man who awaited her with a countenance beaming with love. (4)

Elizabeth Gaskell spells out the point which Dickens implies through stylistic play. The roaring lion text seems to have had particular relevance to the problem of the temptations of the young in the nineteenth century. One of the fathers of modern Unitarianism, Theophilus Lindsey, interpreted the text thus in a sermon: 'The world, at their entrance into it, is continually whispering to the young and gay, by the examples it sets before them, and by the associates they too often meet with; "Come, let us enjoy the present, and let alone serious things and thoughts of another world till to-morrow!" when, alas! to-morrow may never come.'[9] Dickens's comments on Harthouse as the very Devil offer two possible interpretations, one flippant and the other profoundly serious, which, disturbingly, merge in the character's 'What will be, will be' philosophy (II.2).

Like Harthouse, Mrs Sparsit is at once ludicrous and disturbing. Her lively imagination fastens on an appropriate symbol in Louisa's 'mighty Staircase' which she constructs in her mind (II.10). In her eyes, Louisa has only one fate in store: to be led down the Staircase by Harthouse to the 'dark pit of shame and ruin at the bottom'. Other words for 'pit' are equally suggestive of eternal perdition, including 'black gulf' and 'abyss' (II.11), and are as ludicrously hyperbolic. Like Harthouse's devilry, however, Mrs Sparsit's distorted vision of perdition must be examined in the context of the whole novel.

When Mrs Sparsit suspects that Louisa is about to elope with Harthouse, she dashes to the station at Coketown and takes the train out to Bounderby's country house, 'borne along the arches spanning the land of coal-pits past and present' (II.11). She now sees Louisa 'very near the bottom' of the Staircase, on 'the brink of the abyss'. She spies on Louisa and Harthouse in the wood on Bounderby's estate, and jumps to conclusions when she sees Louisa 'hastily cloaked and muffled, and stealing away' from her married home: 'She elopes! She falls from the lowermost stair, and is swallowed up in the gulf.' The description of the rail journey which follows is the authorial narrator's, but it develops the melodramatic scenario of Mrs Sparsit's over-heated imagination. The now soaked Mrs Sparsit, cutting a ludicrous figure with her stained stockings and with caterpillars from the wood slung 'in hammocks of their own making, from various parts of her dress', follows Louisa to the station, where they both wait for the train, listening to the thunder and looking at the lightning: suitable stage effects for the pursuit scene in a lurid melodrama and yet archly suggestive of apocalypse. (There are 'lightnings, and voices, and thunderings, and an earthquake, and great hail' after the last trumpet is sounded (Revelation 11.19).) The train seems a suitable conveyance to the bottomless pit: 'The seizure of the station with a fit of trembling, gradually deepening to a complaint of the heart, announced the train. Fire and steam, and smoke, and red light; a hiss, a crash, a bell, and a shriek; . . . the little station a desert speck in the thunderstorm.' When Mrs Sparsit arrives in Coketown, which is flooded with torrential rain, her vision of judgment is shattered. Rather than eloping with the 'very Devil', Louisa returns to her father at Stone Lodge, as the reader later learns. Far from heralding Louisa's disappearance into the pit, the storm makes a mockery of Mrs Sparsit's detective work. At the end of the chapter she is back in Coketown, having lost track of Louisa, 'with a bonnet like an over-ripe fig' and 'with a stagnant verdure on her general exterior, such as accumulates on an old park fence in a mouldy lane'. In her bitterness she bursts into tears.

The subsequent chapter (II.12: 'Down'), the last in the second book, confirms that the storm mirrors Louisa's inner turmoil, as well as supplying suitable climatic conditions for Mrs Sparsit's stereotyped damnation scene. During the second interview between father and daughter it emerges that Louisa's earlier hints concerning a future breakdown have proved all too prophetic. As rain pours down on Stone Lodge 'like a deluge', Gradgrind is forced to look into the hell of his daughter's mind, thus initiating the judgment on his own values which is the subject of the subsequent book, 'Garnering'. Louisa seems possessed with prophetic fervour:

'What have you done, O father, what have you done, with

the garden that should have bloomed once, in this great wilderness here?'

She struck herself with both her hands upon her bosom.

'If it had ever been here, its ashes alone would save me from the void in which my whole life sinks.'

This outburst is the culmination of long-suppressed emotion. In her despair Louisa invokes the symbols of desolation which have haunted her since early womanhood: 'garden' and 'wilderness', 'ashes' and the 'void'. For her the landscape of pits and fires, black shapes and ashes, and the 'deluge' of the storm, are within. She is 'down' in a way which is reminiscent of Teufelsdrockh's melancholia in the 'Pedagogy' chapter of Carlyle's *Sartor Resartus:* 'The dark bottomless Abyss, that lies under our feet, had yawned open; . . . the inexorable word, NEVER! now first showed its meaning' (II.3).

After the further trials of the third book, in which Tom's crime comes to light, Gradgrind is made doubly certain that he has reaped as he has sown. In the last section of the last chapter ('Final'), where Dickens hints at what will happen in the future, a 'white-haired decrepit' Gradgrind, reminiscent of the old Dombey, is glimpsed 'making his facts and figures subservient to Faith, Hope and Charity' (III.9). As in *Mary Barton*, this kind of 'spirit of Christmas' quoting from New Testament texts has dated badly, seeming maudlin today. The failure of such an allusion to persuade the reader that Dickens is making a substantial contribution to the debate on the Condition of England Question, by advocating that manufacturers and MPs pay closer attention to the New Testament, is as complete as his failure to make Sleary's horse-riding counterbalance Utilitarianism in the dynamical-versus-mechanical debate in the novel. One can imagine, however, that such allusions made a strong emotional appeal to the novel's first readers. Similarly, the grotesqueness of Harthouse's and Mrs Sparsit's egocentric world-views would have stirred many of those readers to thought more effectively than a bushel of Gradgrind's blue books. Louisa's fate is poignantly illustrative of the limitations of Gradgrindery. She is never to be 'again a wife – a mother – lovingly watchful of her children'. Presumably she will continue to stare at the ashes of her fire, 'as in days of yore, though with a gentler and a humbler face' (III.9).

III

'Black and White' was one of Dickens's putative titles for the novel eventually called *Hard Times for These Times.* Whereas the blackness of Gradgrind and Bounderby, and particularly of the former, often shades into grey, even in the early chapters, the whiteness of Stephen the martyr and Rachael the angel is dazzling and unrelieved. Modern readers tend to react unfavourably towards these characters and to the moral heavy artillery which they have on their side, with 'Faith, Hope, and Charity' texts as part of the arsenal. Flitting among the streets of blackened red-brick houses, where the poor man's undertaker plies his black ladder (I.10), Rachael is a visiting Angel in the House to Stephen. Returning home after the re-appearance of his wife, Stephen moves from the 'black wet night' (I.12) into the room where the 'light of her face' shines in 'upon the midnight of his mind' (I.13). Rachael quotes the New Testament as she attempts to calm him: 'Thou knowest who said, "Let him who is without sin among you cast the first stone at her!"' The scene rises to a crescendo of emotionalism when Rachael prevents Stephen's wife from taking poison by accident and Stephen puts the end of her shawl to his lips. Just as Dickens is less impressive when he introduces biblical allusions into his narrative which directly state his own view than when he shows how his characters pervert biblical texts, or subtly implies their blasphemies against the Bible, so his handling of the whiter-than-white Rachael is far less inventive than that of the black or grey characters in the novel. His angel is a stereotype. Although Stephen himself is almost as wooden a character as Rachael, Dickens uses him in a more imaginative way. The two passages in which he is described falling into a pit or, in the first instance, dreaming that he does, are of central importance in their implied symbolic parallels, linking the Louisa plot and the Stephen plot through the use of a landscape of pits and fires.

Stephen dreams two judgment dreams during the troubled night of vigil with Rachael. In the first he is being married to some unknown woman, and the ceremony witnessed by the living and the dead. Darkness comes on, followed by a 'tremendous light' which breaks from 'one line in the table of commandments at the altar', presumably 'Thou shalt not kill' (I.13). The words shine through the church and are 'sounded' too, as if there are 'voices in the fiery letters'. Like Lockwood's second night-mare in *Wuthering Heights*, Stephen's second dream grows out of the first. Everything is changed, except that the clergyman remains with him, standing in the daylight in front of a huge crowd. The millions who stare unpityingly at Stephen seem more numerous than the whole population of the world. (The congregation at the wedding and this crowd are like those which might be gathered on the Day of Judgment: the living and the dead together, and numbering more than the living population of the earth.) A familiar object then takes on a grotesque guise: 'He stood on a raised stage, under his own loom; and, looking up at the shape the loom took, and hearing the burial service distinctly read, he knew that he was there to suffer death. In an instant what he stood on fell below him, and he was gone.' Stephen is oppressed by the staring eyes of the crowds in both dreams, as in his daily life he is an exile, reviled by his work-mates at the mill. His hell on earth, populated by staring crowds, could become an everlasting hell if he commits murder or sits by while his wife accidentally kills herself.

Although the gallows dream proves to have been prophetic when Stephen falls down Old Hell Shaft, the exploration of the 'midnight of his mind', haunted by apocalyptic dreams, is never developed, unlike the analysis of Louisa's morbid sense of alienation. The sixth chapter of 'Garnering', entitled 'The Star-light', opens with Sissy and Rachael walking in the country between Coketown and Bounderby's country house. The land-scape is now described in more detail. A run-down industrial site, the place is dotted with engines at the mouths of old pits, retired working horses, and the ruins of old works. The business of life's transactions has ceased on this Sunday: 'the great wheel of earth seemed to revolve without the shocks and noises of another time' (III.6). Coketown time, measured by Gradgrind's deadly statistical clock, is unheeded in this makeshift playg-round to which weary Coketowners retire for a breath of fresh air. Stephen crosses the dangerous wilderness of industrial ruins at night, hurrying back to Coketown to clear his name, having previously wandered in the wilderness of the unemployed to which he was exiled. The 'chasm', 'pit', or 'gulf' called Old Hell Shaft claims him as its victim. Louisa and Sissy find his cap near the mouth of the shaft, raise the alarm, and then find that time seems to drag as they wait for help to arrive: 'It seemed now hours and hours since she had left the lost man lying in the grave where he had been buried alive.' After a dramatic rescue scene, Stephen describes how he lay in his 'grave' looking up at a star in the sky, thinking it was the one 'as guided to Our Saviour's home'. He is delighted to find that he is to be carried away 'in the direction whither the star seemed to him to lead'. As he is carried through the countryside, it soon becomes a funeral procession. Winched up from the bottom of the pit, Stephen is raised from the dead and ascends into heaven. Cleared of the crime at the bank and innocent of any hurt towards his wife, he is transported to his maker. As I have already suggested, those he leaves behind have to work out their salvations on earth, reviewing their earthly lives and contemplating the future, sometimes dimly perceived, in relation to their conduct. Whereas Louisa's obsession with fire and ashes focuses on the sense of loss associated with the commital of ashes to ashes, Stephen's funeral procession is more suggestive of another passage from the Burial Service and a further variation on the theme of sowing, reaping and garnering: 'It is sown in corruption; it is raised in incorruption' (cf. I Corinthians 15.42).

The Stephen Blackpool plot is handled far less inventively than the Louisa Gradgrind plot, culminating melodramatically in a spirit of Christmas whisking away of the worthy Hand in the manner of Dickens's most maudlin short stories. 'A Child's Dream of a Star', a story published in *Household Words* (6 April 1850) and later in *Reprinted Pieces* (1858), is a particularly interesting precursor of *Hard Times* in this respect. In the opening paragraph, the child and his sister are described *wondering* at everything around them, as Louisa is forbidden to do: 'These two used to wonder all day long. They wondered at the beauty of the flowers; they wondered at the height and blueness of the sky; they wondered at the depth of the bright water; they wondered at the goodness and the power of GOD who made the lovely world' (*Reprinted Pieces*). Louisa echoes the title of Dickens's story in her first interview with her father: 'You have been so careful of me, that I never had a child's heart. You have trained me so well, that I never dreamed a child's dream. You have dealt so wisely with me, father, from my cradle to this hour, that I never had a child's belief or a child's fear' (I.15). Gradgrind's commandment, 'Never Wonder', seems to contradict

Christ's words to his disciples: 'Except ye be converted, and become as little children, ye shall not enter into the kingdom of heaven' (Matthew 18.3). The sister in 'A Child's Dream of a Star' dies young and enters the kingdom of heaven, symbolised as the 'clear shining star' which she and her brother used to wonder at, standing 'hand in hand' at their bedroom window at night. The child now looks at the star with tears in his eyes, but dreams of a 'train of people' taken up the 'sparkling road' of the star's rays by angels. Other members of his family die and follow the same path to the star, while his sister's angel waits for him to join her himself. When he is dying, in old age, he says to those who watch over him: 'My age is falling from me like a garment, and I move towards the star as a child.' The story ends with the star shining upon his grave. It is Stephen's childlike response to the star over Old Hell Shaft which makes his escape from earthly troubles and eternal damnation certain. By setting the rescue in the no man's land between Coketown and Bounderby's house, Dickens achieves a measure of structural unity and draws attention to symbolic parallels between the two plots, but at the cost of making the inequalities of his handling of character and plot glaringly obvious. His sketchy comments on 'wonder' in 'A Child's Dream' give no clue to the remarkable way in which his thoughts on the subject were to be developed in *Hard Times*, whereas the mawkish end of the rescue scene is as crudely emblematic as the earlier story.

IV

Both allusion and symbolism are as wooden as the characters with whom they are associated in Dickens's portrayal of Rachael and Stephen. The allusion to the kissing of the hem of the garment confirms that Rachael is a typical figure, an Angel in the House. Stephen's reference to the star of Bethlehem is as contrived as the resurrection symbolism developed when he is rescued from Old Hell Shaft. In thus suggesting positive virtues in his 'white' characters, Dickens succeeds only in underlining their limitations as stereotypes. In contrast, eschatological allusions associated with other characters provide him with material which he can develop imaginatively, as in his portrayal of Harthouse and Mrs Sparsit, when his true genius is in play. The development of Louisa, the novel's emotional and thematic centre, is handled with a sustained sureness of touch. The subtle inter-relations between apocalyptic allusions and symbolism suggest that her response to Gradgrindery is of more than local importance, representing the instinctive resistance of the human spirit to the 'progress' of a mechanical age towards the 'great public-office Millennium', when Commissioners of Fact should 'reign upon earth'.

Unlike Elizabeth Gaskell in *Mary Barton*, Dickens subsumes allusions into his own rhetoric and, through variations of tone, from the arch to the indignant, from the flippant to the damning, passes judgment on characters and institutions without sacrificing the comic perspective of his novel. It is a measure of Dickens's genius that, of all the novelists I am examining, only he makes both his symbolism and his allusions integral, sometimes almost indistinguishable elements of his distinctive rhetoric, even in a novel which is badly flawed. The articulation of his vision of judgment through eschatological allusions, and the portrayal of landscape and townscape symbolically associated with the Four Last Things, would have baffled none of his readers, vast in number and various in educational background. Louisa's interest in fire and ashes, the landscape of the no man's land, and Harthouse's devilry have common associations which his readers, familiar with biblical, literary and pictorial representations of hell fire, could hardly have missed. *Hard Times* is more than a social-problem novel, for through his use of allusion and symbolism in a work with mainly contemporary social concerns, Dickens opens wide vistas of major thematic importance to all societies.

6

The Spectacles of Books:
Middlemarch

I

Of all Victorian novelists George Eliot is the most demanding in one particular respect. At her best she makes everything in her narrative contribute to the development of her central themes, so that the reader has to concentrate throughout, constantly aware of the fact that an apparently trivial incident or dialogue may prove to be a kind of oblique comment on an important episode elsewhere in the text. This is particularly true of *Middlemarch* (1871–2) in which, to borrow Caleb Garth's words, 'things hang together' in a quite remarkable way (40). George Eliot handles this complex narrative technique most skilfully, and makes allusion a part of that technique most effectively, when portraying the relationship between Dorothea and Casaubon, especially where she relates Casaubon's scholarly aims and methods to the way in which the couple perceive the world and each other.

At the beginning of the novel the myopic pair look at the world and each other through the spectacles of books, in the phrase which Dr Johnson borrowed from Dryden for his *Life of Milton*:

His images and descriptions of the scenes or operations of Nature do not seem to be always copied from original form, nor to have the freshness, raciness, and energy of immediate observation. He saw Nature, as Dryden expresses it, *through the spectacles of books*; and on most occasions calls learning to his assistance.

Casaubon sees everything through the spectacles of books

throughout his life. His methods of research and uses of allusion are related; both are deadening. But Dorothea comes to see her husband's limitations clearly, recognising that her own view of him was idealised before they married. After his death she concentrates less on book-learning and observes the world with the 'freshness' and 'energy' of 'immediate observation'.

George Eliot was clearly aware of the possibilities which allusion offered both as a technique and as a *theme*. She examines the way in which people quote as well as what they quote; and the way in which characters use allusion, at first sight a comparatively unimportant matter, often tells us more about the way in which they think and feel than we might have expected. Before discussing allusion in relation to Casaubon (section III) and Dorothea (III and IV) in detail, I want to re-examine one kind of textual allusion which is particularly important in George Eliot's portrayal of the couple, the shorthand notation, and to consider some of the ways in which it is used by characters in *Middlemarch*.

II

The sturdy inhabitants of Middlemarch and its environs, whether landed gentry, professional people, shopkeepers, or humble cottagers, are keen observers of domestic detail, weighing and measuring their neighbours in terms of those solid artifacts which are indicative of character, wealth and station. Female Middlemarchers are analysts of dress fabrics and bonnets as indicators of social position, and the better off are expert in the intricacies of furnishings and crockery which betray the taste of their owners. The menfolk keep a close eye on the condition of their neighbours' horse-flesh, stabling and fencing. The patronising of Bulstrode's bank and of the Green Dragon is observed and openly discussed. The subjects of George Eliot's 'Study of Provincial Life' are themselves students of that life. Against this background hum of analysis and grading, Lydgate and Farebrother analyse their specimens and Casaubon categorises and indexes the evidence he has accumulated over a period of many years. Meanwhile they themselves are categorised by keen-eyed Middlemarchers.

The better read categorisers in Middlemarch often refer to

types as yardsticks, sometimes using shorthand notations in the
way that Trollope uses them in *Framley Parsonage*: describing a
character (X) as a familiar literary, biblical or mythological
figure (Y) (see p. 21). The casualness of Trollope's references is
typical of thousands of similar shorthand notations in Victorian
fiction in which the qualities associated with the famous characters referred to are scaled down in the new context of a modern,
realistic fictional world. (Such allusions complement Trollope's
masterly art of the low key.) The construction 'X was a Y' can be
particularly reductive, often having a satiric effect, as in mock-
heroic episodes in eighteenth-century novels: X appears to be a
mere shadow of some famous Y. As Y predates X and is assumed
to be familiar to both the writer and contemporary readers of the
novel in which the two are compared, X can appear to be belated
by Y, who is elevated beyond the ken of X. In her handling of
shorthand notations in *Middlemarch*, George Eliot makes the
debunking effect of historical comparisons part of her overall
thematic scheme. What can only be described as an allusive
device in Trollope, employed for fairly insignificant local effects,
is an aspect of George Eliot's highly developed art of allusion in
Middlemarch.

The formidable Mrs Cadwallader uses the cutting shorthand
notation as part of her verbal armoury. Having seen Casaubon
leaving as she entered the grounds of Tipton Grange, she teases
Mr Brooke with these words of greeting as she comes into the
library: 'I see you have had our Lowick Cicero here. . . . I suspect
you and he are brewing some bad politics, else you would not be
seeing so much of the lively man' (6). The obvious irony of 'lively
man' complements the more subtly incongruous suggestion that
Casaubon of 'Low-wick', like Cicero, is both a political
machinator and a great writer and orator. Later, Mrs Cadwallader gleefully seizes on the fact, enjoyed by others as a huge
joke, that Casaubon has sat for Naumann's Aquinas in Rome,
and simply substitutes the name of the pre-eminent theologian
for that of the opinionated cleric who models for his head: 'It is
Aquinas's fault. . . . Why didn't he use his interest to get Ladislaw made an *attaché* or sent to India?' (38). She also uses this
well tried technique on Ladislaw himself, that most elusive of
incomers in Middlemarch, though with slightly less venomous
intent: 'he's a dangerous young sprig, that Mr Ladislaw . . . with
his opera songs and his ready tongue. A sort of Byronic hero – an

amorous conspirator, it strikes me. And Thomas Aquinas is not
fond of him' (38). She later dubs him 'Mr Orlando Ladislaw'
when he is 'making a sad dark-blue scandal' by 'warbling
continually' with Rosamond Lydgate (62). Ladislaw's temporary patron, Mr Brooke, makes several elegant stabs at placing
the young man in his apparently confused mental filing system.
First he tries a few famous examples of what he sees as a specific
type of man: 'He would make a good secretary, now, like
Hobbes, Milton, Swift – that sort of man' (34). His choice of type
changes once Ladislaw is working on the *Pioneer* for him as
editor: ' He seems to me a kind of Shelley, you know'; 'he has the
same sort of enthusiasm for liberty, freedom, emancipation – a
fine thing under guidance' (37). He then sticks to a revised
version of this judgment: 'Mr Brooke always ended by agreeing
with Ladislaw, who still appeared to him a sort of Burke with a
leaven of Shelley' (51). Like the ladies of Middlemarch, Brooke
has an eye for 'receipts'. He also has the maddening habit of
often being closer to the truth in his approximations when
judging others than are many of his fellow judges. (Ladislaw
eventually becomes an 'ardent public man' ('Finale').) By shift-
ing his ground, constantly referring to 'that sort of thing', and
implicating his listeners with a 'you know', Brooke defines only
fields of reference, clusters of examples of types, instinctively
avoiding pinning his man down to one particular precursor in the
manner of Mrs Cadwallader.

The motto on 'classing' a man, presumably written by George
Eliot herself, prefaces her analysis of Bulstrode and the opinion
Middlemarchers have of the banker with the habit of turning a
'moral lantern' on them (13):

> *1st Gent.* How class your man? – as better than the most,
> Or, seeming better, worse beneath that cloak?
> As saint or knave, pilgrim or hypocrite?
> *2nd Gent.* Nay, tell me how you class your wealth of books,
> The drifted relics of all time. As well
> Sort them at once by size and livery:
> Vellum, tall copies, and the common calf
> Will hardly cover more diversity
> Than all your labels cunningly devised
> To class your unread authors.

As in so many passages in *Middlemarch*, the connotations of this motto radiate beyond the local area of reference. The motto not only suggests that Bulstrode is an enigma and hints at the revelations which are to come, but also explicitly focuses attention upon the problem of classing men which is explored elsewhere in the novel. The book analogy brings the libraries of Tipton and Lowick and their respective owners to mind: Brooke with what is probably a miscellaneous but wide-ranging collection of books used in past researches which he decided not to take too far, and Casaubon the student of 'drifted relics' who spends most of his time among his 'dark book-shelves in the long library' at Lowick (9). Casaubon is unwillingly drawn into a discussion of methods of arranging documents when he dines at Tipton at the beginning of the novel. He tells Brooke that he arranges his papers 'in pigeon-holes partly', to which his buoyant host replies: 'Ah, pigeon-holes will not do. I have tried pigeon-holes, but everything gets mixed in pigeon-holes: I never know whether a paper is in A or Z' (2). Like the motto to chapter 13, this passage is of more than local significance, providing oblique commentary on the nature of categorising and of shorthand notations. Whereas Brooke recognises the purpose of a precise method of filing but is incapable of putting it into practice, Casaubon actually works with pigeon-holes, notebooks, and indexes in mind. (Indeed, he can think only in terms of material which can be pigeon-holed as evidence to be cited in his 'Key to all Mythologies'.) Furthermore, Brooke could be describing his own use of shorthand notations and his instinctive recognition that such pigeon-holes have their limitations.

By the end of the novel, Brooke's image as a hopeless muddler is modified in the light of his almost unconsciously shrewd commentary on human affairs. But for the moment Casaubon gravely smiles approval at Dorothea's comment on the issue of pigeon-holes: 'I wish you would let me sort your papers for you, uncle. . . . I would letter them all, and then make a list of subjects under each letter' (2). The perfect amanuensis and research assistant who is to prove so imperfect in Casaubon's eyes, once she is married to him, attracts him now as his eyesight fails. Their mutual attraction is partly based on shared views on such things as arranging documents when they are surrounded by people who seem not to care about or understand such matters.

It is in George Eliot's portrayal of Dorothea comparing her

future husband with his precursors in the early chapters of the
novel that she most successfully adapts the belittling functions of
the shorthand notation to her methods of characterisation. By
contrasting the ways in which Casaubon and Dorothea use
shorthand notations and other kinds of allusion, she indicates
the unbridgeable gap which opens up between them.

III

George Eliot adopts the analogy of quotations when describing
her heroine in the second sentence of her first chapter: her 'profile
as well as her stature and bearing seemed to gain the more
dignity from her plain garments, which by the side of provincial
fashion gave her the impressiveness of a fine quotation from the
Bible, – or from one of our elder poets, – in a paragraph of
to-day's newspaper' (1). Always associated with old things,
Dorothea appears to be of a 'finer' quality than her contemporaries. It is easy to see how this belated Puritan who is known
in Middlemarch as the young lady who sits up at night 'to read
old theological books' (1) is attracted to the owner of autumnal
Lowick, with its 'carpets and curtains with colours subdued by
time, the curious old maps and bird's-eye views on the walls of
the corridor, with here and there an old vase below' (9), whereas
her fashionable sister, Celia, shudders at the thought of living in
such a place with such a man.

When Dorothea sits at table with Casaubon at the beginning
of the novel she idealises what Mrs Cadwallader and others scoff
at: 'His manners, she thought, were very dignified; the set of his
iron-grey hair and his deep eye-sockets made him resemble the
portrait of Locke' (2). After dinner she denies Celia's assertion
that Casaubon is 'very ugly': 'He is one of the most distin-
guished-looking men I ever saw. He is remarkably like the
portrait of Locke. He has the same deep eye-sockets' (2). Celia's
response to this comparison rouses Dorothea's anger:

> 'Had Locke those two white moles with hairs on them?'
> 'Oh, I daresay! when people of a certain sort looked at him,'
> said Dorothea, walking away a little.
> 'Mr Casaubon is so sallow.'
> 'All the better. I suppose you admire a man with the
> complexion of a *cochon de lait*.'

Dorothea is doomed to marry the sallow Casaubon, and Celia is obviously the right wife for the 'blooming', 'red-whiskered' Sir James Chettam. When Dorothea complains that Celia will 'never see the great soul in a man's face', her sister replies, 'not without a touch of naïve malice': 'Has Mr Casaubon a great soul?'

This argument between idealist and realist is renewed immediately before Dorothea announces that she is to marry the man of 'great soul'. She and her sister look at the same man at table but see quite different men. Irritated by his habit of blinking before he speaks, Celia comments: 'I don't know whether Locke blinked, but I'm sure I am sorry for those who sat opposite to him if he did' (5). Dorothea asks her not to make any more 'observations of that kind', but Celia justifies herself by saying that they are 'quite true'. To Dorothea's further objection that 'many things are true which only the commonest minds observe', Celia responds: 'Then I think the commonest minds must be rather useful.' As so often happens in Middlemarch, the common mind observes what the finer mind misses or ignores to its cost. Dorothea is literally and metaphorically short-sighted, seeing only the contours of a face which she can idealise, and missing the white moles. When Mrs Cadwallader later complains that Dorothea must have 'encouraged' the disappointed Sir James Chettam, Celia says: 'Please don't be angry with Dodo; she does not see things' (6).

Dorothea begins to realise that she has viewed Casaubon through the spectacles of books only after she is married to him. George Eliot describes her 'very childlike ideas about marriage' before she and Casaubon are drawn together: 'She felt sure that she would have accepted the judicious Hooker, if she had been born in time to save him from that wretched mistake he made in matrimony; or John Milton when his blindness had come on; or any of the other great men whose odd habits it would have been glorious piety to endure' (1). Ironically, the epithet 'judicious' was applied to Hooker by Sir William Cowper in an epitaph in which he wrote of Hooker's 'lasting monument / In his own books', a monument of the kind which Casaubon fails to leave. The epitaph is quoted at the end of the Life of Hooker (1665) in which Walton makes the dubious claim that the great man married the wrong woman because he was credulous and weak-willed. Dorothea begins to know Casaubon as he really is, and thus to see that she may have made a wretched mistake in matrimony herself, in Rome, where the honeymoon centres upon her husband's studies in the Vatican library: 'How far the judicious Hooker or any other hero of erudition would have been the same at Mr Casaubon's time of life, she had no means of knowing, so that he could not have the advantage of comparison; but her husband's way of commenting on the strangely impressive objects around them had begun to affect her with a sort of mental shiver' (20). She now hears what she could not see before. Casaubon is like Milton only in the fact that he has to 'use the utmost caution' about his eyesight (2). Even he can see that Dorothea's image of herself reading Latin and Greek aloud to him, 'as Milton's daughters did to their father, without understanding what they read', is idealistic, and points out in his stilted way what she ignores: that the daughters 'regarded that exercise in unknown tongues as a ground for rebellion against the poet' (7).

Like her uncle, Dorothea has in mind a composite picture of a particular type, in her case the learned writer, when she uses shorthand notations. Locke, Hooker and Milton are joined by Pascal in the hall of fame which her Casaubon is to enter one day: 'There would be nothing trivial about our lives. Everyday-things with us would mean the greatest things. It would be like marrying Pascal' (3). The turning-point in Pascal's life was a spiritual vision which he recorded in a famous written account, after which he dedicated his life to God, necessarily eschewing any possibility of marriage. Casaubon is also 'a living Bossuet, whose work would reconcile complete knowledge with devoted piety; here was a modern Augustine who united the glories of doctor and saint' (3). Like most of the figures to whom Dorothea compares Casaubon, both the 'doctor *and* saint' and Bossuet, the seventeenth-century churchman *and* controversialist, were influential not only through their writings but also through their work outside the study. Living in the era of reform which followed in the wake of the Industrial Revolution in England and the Napoleonic Wars in Europe, Casaubon is untouched by the sense of change and development registered by even the worst educated in Middlemarch. He is desk-bound and writes nothing influential at his desk. Perhaps the only characteristics which do genuinely link him with many of Dorothea's heroes of erudition are the bad health which he shares with Hooker, Locke and Pascal, and the weak eyesight which makes him a latter-day

Milton. Casaubon merely has the 'spare form and the pale complexion' which becomes a student (2) and which Dorothea thinks dignified. This general observation on the 'student' is developed through the Burton motto which prefaces chapter 5, in which Casaubon sends his dryasdust letter of proposal to Dorothea:

> 'Hard students are commonly troubled with gowts, catarrhs, rheums, cachexia, bradypepsia, bad eyes, stone, and collick, crudities, oppilations, vertigo, winds, consumptions, and all such diseases as come by over-much sitting: they are most part lean, dry, ill-coloured . . . and all through immoderate pains and extraordinary studies. If you will not believe the truth of this, look upon great Tostatus and Thomas Aquainas' works; and tell me whether those men took pains.'
> – BURTON'S *Anatomy of Melancholy*, P.I, s.2.

The links between poor health and the labours of scholarship are obvious to all observers of the owner of Lowick, that 'melancholy' house (9). Pathetically, no other parallels between Casaubon and the eminent men referred to by Dorothea suggest themselves.

I have called Dorothea's heroes, Casaubon's precursors in her eyes, learned writers. The parallel between Casaubon and a formidable *scholar* who, in Burton's terms, took 'immoderate pains' over the more pedantic aspects of his 'extraordinary studies', is George Eliot's: 'His very name carried an impressiveness hardly to be measured without a precise chronology of scholarship' (1). Although Meric Casaubon was not unlike the *Middlemarch* character in certain respects, George Eliot is presumably referring to his more famous father, Isaac (1559–1614), who published prodigious quantities of scholarly work at the expense of his health and was involved in the English politics of the day. Few of George Eliot's readers would have known enough about Isaac Casaubon to be able to draw close comparisons between him and the fictional character. (Such comparisons tend to lead to speculation on Eliot's sources rather than her use of the name as a kind of allusion.[1]) Her naming of the character and her comment on the name simply complement the recurrent pattern of generalised and idealised comparison which is later undermined. Thomas Browne comments on the typing of men early in the First Part of *Religio Medici* (1642) in a way which Dorothea would have appreciated: 'Every man is not only himself; there hath been many Diogenes, and as many Timons, though but few of that name: men are liv'd over again, the world is now as it was in Ages past; there was none then, but there hath been some one since that parallels him, and is, as it were, his revived self.' Contrariwise, Casaubon *is* of that name but is not the prolific Isaac's revived self.

The ways in which Casaubon himself uses allusion reflect his habits of work and his limitations as a scholar. During the early days of what passes for his courtship of Dorothea, she becomes convinced that her first impressions were just: 'He was all she had at first imagined him to be: almost everything he had said seemed like a specimen from a mine, or the inscription on the door of a museum which might open on the treasures of past ages' (3). Casaubon's words, inscription-like in their allusive derivativeness, ironically suggest galleries of *dead* material behind them. Dorothea mistakes Casaubon's ability to pigeon-hole, index, or label his museum pieces (material inherited from past writers) for the ability to recognise and preserve 'treasures'. Casaubon is always ready to supply neatly catalogued parallels from his store of learning in any kind of conversation, thus implying that all discourse is somehow redundant. Dorothea finds that he can 'mention historical examples before unknown to her' when discussing the spiritual religion expressed in 'the best Christian books of widely-distant ages' (3). But he also usually assents to her more personal 'expressions of devout feeling' with 'an appropriate quotation', suggestive of a measure of intellectual distance at such intimate moments. He hardly notices the treasures of Rome. What is 'fresh' to Dorothea's mind is 'worn out to his' (20). He can only cite the opinion of others on works of art, Raphael being 'the painter who has been held to combine the most complete grace of form with sublimity of expression', or so at least he has gathered to be 'the opinion of cognoscenti' (20). Dorothea's later disappointment in her husband's inability to share ideas which excite her is described by George Eliot in terms of his use of the deadening reference:

If she spoke with any keenness of interest to Mr Casaubon, he heard her with an air of patience as if she had given a quotation from the Delectus [a Classics primer] familiar to him from his

tender years, and sometimes mentioned curtly what ancient
sects or personages had held similar ideas, as if there were too
much of that sort in stock already. (37)

(Hiram Ford is Casaubon's polar opposite when he shouts a
defiance which he does not know to be Homeric at Fred Vincy in
the hay-field (56).) For the failed author of the 'Key to all
Mythologies', everything seems to be *déjà vu*.

Physically ill, short-sighted and, one assumes, impotent,
Casaubon's responses to the physical world around him are
almost extinct. Pathetically, his explorations of his chosen mental world in the libraries at Lowick and the Vatican are equally
sterile. Rather than emerging from his years of research the
discoverer of a new synthesis of old materials, he is merely
weighed down by those materials. Hence the habitual references
to historical examples, the appropriate quotations, and the lack
of spontaneity in his response to ideas. He has always made
abstracts, or summaries, of what he has read, probably because
the recording of an argument for future use, usually to prove that
there is no new thing under the sun, has been more important to
him than his own imaginative or intellectual response to the work
itself. According to Mrs Cadwallader, 'They say, when he was a
little boy, he made an abstract of "Hop o' my Thumb," and he
has been making abstracts ever since' (8). Dorothea helps
Casaubon in the work of compiling and categorising specimens
of old sources at Lowick and thus 'sees' clearly for the first time
in the novel. I can best illustrate this by analysing in some detail
a pivotal chapter (29) in the development of their relationship. It
is here that the various uses of allusion discussed above conspire
to expose Casaubon's limitations with devastating effect, when
the collector of dead materials has his first brush with death.

The chapter opens with a pointed reminder of the earlier
arguments between Dorothea and Celia. George Eliot states that
Casaubon is 'spiritually a-hungered like the rest of us', in spite of
the 'blinking eyes and white moles objectionable to Celia'. He
marries because the world is getting dimmer and he feels lonely.
By marrying he can acquire a constant companion and helpmate,
and hopes to leave behind him a 'copy of himself'. Copies of
himself, like copies of the Key, are not to be forthcoming, of
course. The 'Parerga' which have appeared, 'small monumental
records of his march', received little attention among scholarly

circles apart from 'that depreciatory recension which was kept locked in a small drawer of Mr Casaubon's desk', probably written by his old acquaintance, Carp of Brasenose. By filing the document in this way he hopes to bury it. Typically, now that he is preparing another Parergon he seems to be concentrating on organising the *referential* material which he will need. He does, however, have to write part of the text:

> References were extensive even here, but not altogether shoreless; and sentences were actually to be written in the shape wherein they would be scanned by Brasenose and a less formidable posterity. These minor monumental productions were always exciting to Mr Casaubon; digestion was made difficult by the interference of citations, or by the rivalry of dialectical phrases ringing against each other in his brain.

Casaubon becomes animated only when faced with the prospect of assembling a suitable battery of references and citations, linked with his own desiccated prose, with which to fend off potential criticisms from the audience which lurks in the shadows. The unmarked Browne quotation ('minor monuments' in *Urn-burial* (see p. 4 above)) implies that this Parergon is a relic even as it is written and will be buried as soon as it is published, being on an outdated subject and full of references to earlier sources. Casaubon can find some consolation in the fact that future generations of scholars will find the Parergon more difficult to assess in terms of originality when they 'exhume' it than will his contemporaries at Brasenose.

The work assigned to Dorothea, 'reading aloud or copying', is designed to help Casaubon in his preparation of the abstracts and references which will make up the bulk of his Parergon. On the morning of the chapter, Casaubon is obviously in a 'foggy' mood. His severe comments on Ladislaw's proposal to visit Lowick and his premature judgment of Dorothea's response to this 'distraction' is a 'sharp sting': 'Dorothea had thought that she could have been patient with John Milton, but she had never imagined him behaving in this way.' The real proves to be far less manageable than the ideal. She startles her husband by objecting strongly to his presuppositions. When he returns to his writing, having demanded that no more be said on the subject, his hand trembles so much that the words seem to be 'written in an unknown character'. Dorothea's writing also changes, but in quite the reverse way. Far from finding her hands trembling as she writes out *quotations* which have been given to her the day before, she feels that she is 'forming her letters beautifully' and seems to see the 'construction of the Latin' she is copying 'more clearly than usual'. The life ebbs from Casaubon as Dorothea, asserting herself and beginning to renounce the role of helpmate, grows stronger and more confident. George Eliot echoes the Milton/Casaubon parallels of earlier chapters for the second time in chapter 29 when she quotes from the passage in *Paradise Lost* which she used as the motto to chapter 3: 'In her indignation there was a sense of superiority, but it went out for the present in firmness of stroke, and did not compress itself into an inward articulate voice pronouncing the once "affable archangel" a poor creature.'[2] The phrase 'for the present' suggests what is to come. Casaubon of the white moles and short temper is no Locke, no Milton, and no Raphael (*Paradise Lost*, VII. 41). As Dorothea grows in knowledge and understanding of her Latin and her spouse, the little self-esteem left in the anxious scholar withers away.

Casaubon's heart-attack half an hour later is the product of grinding toil as one of Burton's hard students over a long period, and of the tension caused by this sudden clash between scholar and wife-cum-research-assistant. It is specifically a scholar's attack, striking Casaubon when he is on the library-steps and making him drop a book with a loud bang on the floor. Again, as Casaubon weakens, here rehearsing his death, Dorothea's strength and energy seem all the greater: 'She *started up* and *bounded* towards him in an instant: he was evidently in great straits for breath. *Jumping* on a stool she got close to his elbow' (my emphasis). Significantly, it is Lydgate who is sent for and who comes 'wonderfully soon'. So begins a relationship which is to develop only after Casaubon's subsequent death. As the younger generation (Lydgate, Sir James and Celia) gather round the young Dorothea at the end of the chapter, the prematurely aged scholar seems as good as dead.

This chapter is pivotal both in the development of Dorothea's relationship with Casaubon and in the exploration of the major themes associated with that relationship. Casaubon has been associated with death from the first. During the dinner party at Tipton, he himself admits that he lives 'too much with the dead' and that his 'mind is something like the ghost of an ancient, wandering about the world and trying mentally to construct it as it used to be, in spite of ruin and confusing changes' (2). Dorothea's two potential younger husbands are both revolted by the idea of Casaubon's marriage to Dorothea. To Sir James he is 'no better than a mummy' (6) and to Ladislaw he has 'no business to be luring a girl into his companionship' if he has chosen to 'grow grey crunching bones in a cavern' (37). Ladislaw's blunt exposure of his belatedness as a scholar, 'groping about in woods with a pocket-compass' while the Germans have made 'good roads' (21), prepares us for the pun in Casaubon's reference to his 'late tractate' (37) – recent, belated (or out of date), and deceased – and for the pathos of George Eliot's description of him 'carrying his taper among the tombs of the past' while Carp & Company come athwart the 'dim light', and interrupt his 'diligent exploration' (42). The deadening quality of his allusions and methods of work is captured in an episode in Rome when Dorothea accompanies him to the Vatican, walking 'through the stony avenue of inscriptions' and parting with him at the entrance to the library (20), for we know that he walks through similar avenues of the mind within the library. He is soon to look into the eyes of death at Lowick when pacing up and down that avenue of living trees fit for a graveyard, the Yew-Tree Walk (42). Here are no historical examples, abstracts of classical authorities, or stony inscriptions to fall back on. Instead the 'commonplace "We must all die"', familiar to educated and uneducated alike, transforms itself into the 'acute consciousness "I must die – and soon"'.

IV

The contrast between Casaubon's scholarly aims and uses of allusion and those of his young wife is akin to the contrast between what St Paul calls the 'letter' and the 'spirit' of the new testament:

> [God] also hath made us able ministers of the new testament; not of the letter, but of the spirit: for the letter killeth, but the spirit giveth life.
> But if the ministration of death, written and engraven in

stones, was glorious, so that the children of Israel could not
stedfastly behold the face of Moses for the glory of his
countenance; which glory was to be done away:

How shall not the ministration of the spirit be rather
glorious?

(II Corinthians 3.6–8)

Whereas Casaubon fixes all his attention on the 'letter', on that
which can be 'written and engraven in stones', Dorothea always
responds to the 'spirit' of what she reads and tries to do useful
work in the same spirit.[3]

This contrast is sharply defined in the first book of the novel,
'Miss Brooke', in which the 'later-born' Theresa (Prelude) decides that she will devote her life to Casaubon, the great soul. It is
instructive to return to her inner thoughts on Casaubon as a
Pascal, mentioned earlier:

Everyday-things with us would mean the greatest things. It
would be like marrying Pascal. I should learn to see the truth
by the same light as great men have seen it by. And then I
should know what to do, when I got older: I should see how it
was possible to lead a grand life here – now – in England. I
don't feel sure about doing good in any way now . . . unless it
were building good cottages – there can be no doubt about
that. (3)

Notice the sequence of thoughts here, from seeing the truth
through marrying a great man to *knowing what to do*, and thus
leading a grand life. For the present she is frustrated in her desire
to be of use, even in the smallest way, being too late to improve
the cottages at Lowick, which have already been attended to. It is
on this very issue that Casaubon gives her sole cause for disappointment at this stage: 'Mr Casaubon apparently did not care
about building cottages, and diverted the talk to the extremely
narrow accommodation which was to be had in the dwellings of
the ancient Egyptians, as if to check a too high standard' (3).
Whereas Casaubon cites sources in order to close off areas of
human activity, Dorothea wants to draw on sources for intellectual or moral guidance on ways of living and for justification for
putting some theory into practice. Whereas Casaubon emerges
from his studies with a sense that everything in the present is

déjà vu, Dorothea's constant concern is with the here-and-now in relation to an idealised future:

> How could she be confident that one-roomed cottages were not for the glory of God, when men who knew the classics appeared to conciliate indifference to the cottages with zeal for the glory? Perhaps even Hebrew might be necessary – at least the alphabet and a few roots – in order to arrive at the core of things, and judge soundly on the social duties of the Christian. (7)

Of course, Dorothea is naïve in thinking that the alphabet and a few roots can help her to arrive at the core of things. But although this 'core' eludes her, the search is valuable in itself. Casaubon's search for his 'key' leads to a literal and metaphorical graveyard. If Dorothea had written a book 'she must have done it as Saint Theresa did, under the command of an authority that constrained her conscience' (10). She does not want to 'deck herself with knowledge', to 'wear it loose from the nerves and blood' that feed her action.

Marriage to Casaubon threatens to drain Dorothea both of energy and of the will to apply knowledge rather than 'wear it loose'. We learn that she 'knew many passages of Pascal's *Pensées* and of Jeremy Taylor by heart' before she was married (1). The *Pensées* and Taylor's *Holy Living* and *Holy Dying* lend themselves to gnomic quotation and to application, being more concerned with Christian ethics than with theological theory. During one of her worst periods of ennui as Casaubon's wife, on the afternoon following his snubbing of Ladislaw during morning service, Dorothea turns to the little heap of favourite books with which she usually occupies herself on Sunday afternoons, from Herodotus, which she is learning to read with Casaubon, to 'her old companion Pascal, and Keble's "Christian Year"' (48). The Herodotus is evidence of her continued attempts to educate herself in the Classics; the Pascal is an old friend; the Keble is the recent (1827) collection of 'Thoughts in Verse for the Sundays and Holydays throughout the Year', some of which were sung as hymns, which became standard Sunday reading. Both scholarship and Christian literature fail to stimulate her today:

She opened one after another, and could read none of them.

Everything seemed dreary: the portents before the birth of
Cyrus – Jewish antiquities – oh dear! – devout epigrams – the
sacred chime of favourite hymns – all alike were as flat as
tunes beaten on wood.

Unable to share with Casaubon either the intimacies of her
spiritual life or her love of the lyrical qualities ˄ᶠ ˡiterature (at
Lowick a solitary harpsichord is covered with books (7)),
Dorothea seems as dreary as Mariana in her moated grange,
even though a husband dozes in the library.

These references to Dorothea's reading are important in their
context (48), for it is in this chapter that she specifically compares Casaubon with Ladislaw and then finds him dead in the
summer-house. She is 'hungering' for 'a fuller sort of companionship' than Casaubon can offer. Whereas everything at Lowick, including some of her favourite books, seems dead, Ladislaw
represents life and fertility:

She longed for work which would be directly beneficent like
the sunshine and the rain, and now it appeared that she was to
live more and more in a virtual tomb, where there was the
apparatus of a ghastly labour producing what would never see
the light. To-day she had stood at the door of the tomb and
seen Will Ladislaw receding into the distant world of warm
activity and fellowship – turning his face towards her as he
went.

Many men would suggest a distant world of warm activity
when seen from the door of such a tomb. Dorothea's view of
Ladislaw can be no more objective than her earlier, idealised view
of Casaubon, being strongly influenced by the condition of the
light and her angle of vision.

In the evening, Casaubon persuades Dorothea to help begin
the process of sifting through his material for the Key as a
preliminary to actually writing the book. The work continues
during a wakeful period in the night. Casaubon seems remarkably alert and decisive as he rapidly surveys ground he has
been creeping over for years. When he asks her to promise to
continue work on the Key after his death she says she needs a day
in which to make up her mind, picturing to herself 'the days, and
months, and years which she must spend in sorting what might

be called shattered mummies, and fragments of a tradition which was itself a mosaic wrought from crushed ruins'. After a night of anxiety and broken sleep, she rises to hear that Casaubon is to take a turn in the Yew-Tree Walk where he hopes to hear her answer. She is weary and afraid, sensing that she will say '"Yes" to her own doom'. The words of her faithful old servant, Tantripp, addressed to Casaubon's butler, prove to be prophetic: 'I wish every book in that library was built into a caticom [sic] for your master.' But the rummaging among tombs and catacombs, avenues of stony inscriptions and old libraries is over, for Casaubon has walked through the Yew-Tree Walk to the summer-house, where Dorothea finds him slumped over a stone table.

Casaubon has imagined that Dorothea would work on the Key after his death. Thus she would erect a 'tomb with his name upon it' (50) in George Eliot's phrase. But the months have gained on him and left his plans 'belated'. He also planned to control her life by means of the 'dead hand' of his will, debarring her from her inheritance in the event of her marrying Will Ladislaw. Both plans are unfulfilled, and for similar reasons.

In the first chapter of Book Six ('The Widow and the Wife') the June sun 'gazes' into the library in the mornings, shining on the 'rows of note-books as it shines on the weary waste planted with huge stones, the mute memorial of a forgotten faith' (54). She carefully seals the *'Synoptical Tabulation for the use of Mrs Casaubon'* left for her by her husband, writing inside the envelope: *'I could not use it. Do you not see now that I could not submit my soul to yours, by working hopelessly at what I have no belief in? – Dorothea.'* The conflicts which have defined the relationship are still implied: stone versus nerves and blood, dead antiquity versus the here-and-now, forgotten faith versus living belief, the letter versus the spirit. Dorothea deposits the paper in her own desk, burying Casaubon's document as Casaubon buried Carp's.

Ladislaw's ambition, stated with contempt by Casaubon near the beginning of the novel, was to 'go abroad again, without any special object, save the vague purpose of what he calls culture, preparation for he knows not what' (9), whereas Casaubon himself travels only for a narrow purpose, cannot respond to great art, and falls into the fatal trap of pre-judging the results of his research, having too decided an aim for which he only prepares. The turning-point for the widowed Dorothea comes when she discards her deepest mourning, having had a vision which, like Ladislaw's early ambition, prepares her for she knows not what. The short-sightedness of her earlier, book-centred life hardly troubles her as she draws the curtains and looks out beyond the entrance-gates after an anguished night spent thinking about her discovery of Ladislaw with Rosamond (80). She can see 'a man with a bundle on his back and a woman carrying her baby'. The figures moving in the field are harder to distinguish: '*perhaps* the shepherd with his dog' (my emphasis). But her 'vision' is strong: 'Far off in the bending sky was the pearly light; and she felt the largeness of the world and the manifold wakings of men to labour and endurance. She was a part of that involuntary, palpitating life, and could neither *look out* on it from her luxurious shelter as a mere *spectator*, nor hide her *eyes* in selfish complaining' (my emphasis). After this moment of vision, Dorothea has a new resolve to achieve 'some-thing', as yet indistinct, but is haunted by the tradition that 'fresh garments' belong to all 'initiation'. What to Casaubon would have been a fragment of evidence for his study of mythologies is sharply alive to his young widow.

The Saturday morning on which she and Ladislaw are brought together begins with practical difficulties for Dorothea (83). She has visited Rosamond, has had two nights of sound sleep, and now has 'a great deal of superfluous strength'. But the villagers seem to need no help. In the brown library she finds that she cannot concentrate on her 'particular little heap of books on political economy and kindred matters', out of which she is trying to 'get light as to the best way of spending money so as not to injure one's neighbours'. Her mind wanders off the subject for a whole hour. She reads sentences twice over without taking in a word. Having wandered round the library, she peruses a map of Asia Minor, but fails to remember the difficult place-names she is trying to fix in her memory. It is important that Will comes to her in the library, the scene of her former imprisonment, where 'her husband's prohibition' seems to dwell. When they stand looking out of the library window at the storm, as suggestive of change and initiation as the fresh garments of the earlier chapter, Dorothea has turned her back on the rows of note-books, has put off the spectacles of books, in order to see nature in turmoil with the freshness of immediate observation: evergreens with the 'pale underside of their leaves against the blackened sky', and flashes of lightning, suggestive of apocalypse. With touching simplicity, Dorothea gives up Lowick and faces her new life with the last words of the chapter: 'I will learn what everything costs.'

The marriages among the younger generation (Dorothea and Ladislaw, Mary Garth and Fred Vincy) with which the novel closes are love-matches. The engagement of Mary to Fred is garlanded with a chapter motto from Hugo's *L'Homme qui rit*, in which the mummifying metaphor earlier applied to Casaubon has new connotations: '*Le coeur se sature d'amour comme d'un sel divin qui le conserve; de là l'incorruptible adhérence de ceux qui se sont aimés dès l'aube de la vie, et la fraîcheur des vieilles amours prolongés. Il existe un embaumement d'amour*' (86). New life has followed death; 'Sunset' (Book Eight) has given way to 'Sunrise'; autumn to spring. Embalming suggests lasting sweetness in the life of Fred and Mary where once it meant only death-in-life for Casaubon and Dorothea. However, Dorothea's life with Ladislaw, the 'ardent public man' and reformer, is still to be pathetically limited in scope, being merely supportive: 'Many who knew her, thought it a pity that so substantive and rare a creature should have been absorbed into the life of another, and be only known in a certain circle as a wife and mother' ('Finale'). The 'new Theresa' is a belated figure in the nineteenth century, having no opportunity to reform a 'conventual life'. George Eliot closes her penultimate paragraph with a warning that 'we insignificant people with our daily words and acts are preparing the lives of many Dorotheas, some of which may present a far sadder sacrifice than that of the Dorothea whose story we know'. We have seen that Casaubon was like the famous Isaac Casaubon in terms of scholarly toil, ill health, and name, but that he could not emulate his precursor in his published work. Here we see Dorothea being discussed as a type in her own right, there being many Dorotheas. Dorothea is thus more firmly placed in her own century as a modern type of woman, whereas Casaubon's very name seem archaic.

The ending of *Middlemarch* is sombre and yet ambiguous:[4]

The effect of her being on those around her was incalculably diffusive: for the growing good of the world is partly dependent on unhistoric acts; and that things are not so ill with you and me as they might have been, is half owing to the number who lived faithfully a hidden life, and rest in unvisited tombs.

Like *Hard Times*, George Eliot's novel ends with a statement which implicates reader and writer in its concerns and which focuses on death, awaiting reader, writer, and character alike. The effect of the spirit is incalculably diffusive. Unhistoric acts remain unrecorded, are not set down in letters. The epitaph written on an unvisited tomb remains unread. Dorothea's life with her husband and son (the new heir of Lowick, now that Dorothea has slipped out of the grasp of the dead hand) is at once life-enhancing and unhistoric, and thus well below her own high expectations. Tragically, she is to Theresa what Casaubon is to Locke. Yet she has had her vision. Lifting her eyes from her books, setting aside the spectacles of books, she has seen what others are incapable of seeing.

V

Several Victorian critics of *Middlemarch* complained that it was too obviously the work of an intellectual; that it was too overtly analytical. One critic stated that George Eliot tells us beforehand 'what is going on in the speaker's mind, analysing the whole process to the utter destruction of that charm and apparent unconsciousness and consequent surprise and credence which makes us feel that we are not assisting at a got-up show, but living an experience'.[5] Another wrote: 'If we have a fault to find in *Middlemarch*, it is that it is almost *too* laboured. Good as are the points, and telling as is their humour, they yet show far too clearly the *labor limae* [labour of revision].'[6] The reviewer in the *Spectator* (1872) commented on the general reception of the novel: 'We all grumble at *Middlemarch*; we all say that the action is slow, that there is too much parade of scientific and especially physiological knowledge in it, that there are turns of phrase which are even pedantic . . . ; but we all read it.'[7]

Some passages in the novel, especially in the chapters devoted to Lydgate and his research, certainly seem too close to George Eliot's 'quarries'.[8] Although many of the allusions I have discussed are also the product of her quarrying among sources, particularly seventeenth-century sources, they are not obscure and do not seem to be part of a 'got-up show'. This is largely because many of these allusions are Casaubon's and Dorothea's rather than the authorial narrator's, and for both characters, books are familiars and learned references a commonplace feature of discourse. Thus George Eliot's art of allusion is at once most sophisticated and undemonstrative in her parallel explorations of the relationships between Casaubon and Dorothea, and between both characters and their books. As she reveals the neuroses of the couple and analyses their different ways of perceiving the world, with Casaubon distancing it and Dorothea trying to act in it, literary quotations and references are experienced rather than merely recognised by the reader, being part of the fabric (or 'web') of Middlemarch life. The underlying theme of the idealisation and distortion of reality when seen through the spectacles of books makes apparently disparate 'things hang together' in the novel (40). Allusion, the meaningful bringing together of what are otherwise discrete and unrelated fragments of literature, is therefore of central importance, both as a technique and a theme, in the complex literary synthesis that is *Middlemarch*.

7

The Bower and the World: *The Egoist*

I

In terms of the changing relationship between novelists and their readers in the Victorian age, George Eliot was a transitional writer. Although her comparatively difficult novels were surprisingly popular with the public, it has been suggested that self-improving readers may have stuck to their task through a sense of duty, without always fully understanding what they read.[1] The first major Victorian novelist to be consistently *attacked* for his difficulty and obscurity, and to resist the pressure of this criticism, was George Meredith.

As a novelist, Meredith was always concerned with the principles of his art, never with his role as a novelist writing for a wide reading public. In a letter of January 1862, addressed to Augustus Jessopp, he reminds his correspondent that 'Pater familias has given Mr. Mudie a very large bit of his petticoated mind' concerning him, and comments: 'In the way of Art I never stop to consider what is admissible to the narrow minds of the drawing-room.'[2] Meredith not only mocked contemporary readers for their prudishness but was said to have inveighed against what he called the 'porkers' (the public) in general.[3] Oscar Wilde, for whose writing Meredith cleared a path, seems to have sympathised with the novelist's attitude towards a gross reading public. The exquisite Vivian in 'The Decay of Lying' (1889) says of him: 'He has refused to bow the knee to Baal, and after all, even if the man's fine spirit did not revolt against the noisy assertions of realism, his style would be quite sufficient of itself to keep life at a respectful distance.' Meredith's style certainly kept many

100

readers at a disrespectful distance from his novels. Although *The Egoist* (1879) marked the turning point in his writing career and was the novel which first brought him real critical acclaim, the comments of a contemporary reviewer in the *Examiner* are typical:

> Obscurity, we can assure Mr Meredith, is not necessarily interesting. And want of intelligibility disfigures, unfortunately, more than the mere Prelude of *The Egoist*. The author will probably say that the reader's stupidity is in fault; but we submit that novelists do not write only for persons who are preternaturally acute in filling up elisions and elucidating *variorum* readings.[4]

The reviewer in the *Saturday Review* (1879) doubted whether the novel would 'much widen Mr Meredith's public', partly because 'the book must be read, not page by page like the ordinary novel, but line by line'.[5] Few would now argue that the text of *The Egoist* does not merit a line by line reading. One wonders, however, how many readers, both Victorian and modern, have been deterred from even tackling the main text of a novel which has an extremely difficult Prelude, written in clotted Carlylese.

Meredith is one of the most 'allusive' of all nineteenth-century novelists. Like his style and his symbolism, however, many of his literary allusions in *The Egoist* are less accessible than those of his Victorian precursors. Although the narrative does contain networks of allusions of the kind I have examined in previous chapters, they are difficult even to discern on a first reading. (R. L. Stevenson was surely not alone in finding that the richness of the novel could be savoured only after a number of readings.) Moreover, the general 'allusiveness' of the novel is closer in kind to the adaptive stategies Moler finds in Jane Austen (see p. 19 above) than it is to the thematic and structural functions of quotations and references which I have discussed hitherto. Indeed, Moler's description of Austen's 'borrowings' from the 'common stock', the 'manipulation of one, or perhaps a combination of several traditional motifs, character types, situations, or themes', could be applied to Meredith's play with conventions in *The Egoist*.

The first half of my discussion is an analysis of this different kind of allusiveness in the novel, and focuses on Meredith's handling of allusion, both as a technique and as a theme, in his portrayal of Sir Willoughby's circle of friends and relations in Patterne Hall. I then move on to examine a specific set of classical references which function as thematic pointers in the part of the narrative in which Meredith develops the contrasts between this closed circle and the outer world, through the symbolism associated with the cherry-tree in the park. As a wooer, Sir Willoughby offers Clara Middleton an 'enclosed and fortified bower' of Egoism, but discovers that she is unwilling to 'spurn the world', or to 'kick the world' out of that bower (6). Each of the major characters in the novel takes up a different stance in relation to the world outside Patterne Hall. Their walking habits are one of several indications of these stances: Vernon Whitford is a keen alpinist and takes long walks in the countryside surrounding the Hall, whereas Sir Willoughby prefers to ride within easy reach of the house, displaying his 'leg' to advantage, and walks willingly only when he parades with the ladies on the terrace, there to repel boarders in the shape of Lieutenants of Marines; Clara likes fields and commons, whereas Laetitia Dale favours enclosed parks. The statuesque Sir Willoughby is anxious to keep Vernon, Clara and Laetitia around him. Vernon acts as his secretary and writes on classical authors on his behalf. Clara 'completes' him. Laetitia is his 'mirror', and mirrors are useful only if they remain still. In Sir Willoughby's eyes, London is the 'burial-place of the individual man' (4), and Vernon's plan to move to London troubles him:

> You can have one of my cottages, or a place built for you. Anything to keep a man from destroying the sense of stability about one. In London, my dear old fellow, you lose your identity. What are you there? I ask you, what? One has the feeling of the house crumbling when a man is perpetually for shifting and cannot fix himself. (11)

Sir Willoughby's sense of a loss of stability is to be a central theme in the chapters which follow. Patterned porcelain is to be shattered and rules of etiquette broken. His second fiancée is to bolt from the house and across the park to the fields beyond, during a storm. Finally he is to return to the woman whom he formerly embraced as the mirror of himself, Laetitia, only to discover that she is no longer willing to be a mirror and dictates the terms on which their marriage is to be based. Clara is to escape to the Alps with her beloved Vernon. The simple plot of betrothals and jiltings provides a framework within which Meredith explores relations between the inner self and the outer 'clothed' self, and between the 'bower' of Patterne Hall and the 'world' which is to be discovered beyond its gates.

II

Although Sir Willoughby himself gave up the Classics for more modish science, he likes his cousin, Vernon Whitford, to date his controversial writings on classical subjects from Patterne Hall, thus giving the house 'a flavour of a bookish aristocracy' (10). Like Vernon's classical writings, the witty exchanges in conversations at the Hall allay Sir Willoughby's fears concerning the gross world breaking into his circle, for the house appears to be linguistically as well as topographically remote from that world. Meredith's characters are combatants in frequent battles of wits and words, and each has his or her own verbal arsenal. Vernon has his epigrams and Horace de Craye his aphorisms (10, 18). Sir Willoughby has a wide range of weapons, being a 'polished whisperer, a lively dialoguer, one for witty bouts, with something in him . . . beyond mere wit', as they soon learn who call up his 'reserves' and have a 'bosom for pinking' (17). Mrs Mountstuart Jenkinson, a benevolent Mrs Cadwallader,[6] is the *grande dame* of the circle, refereeing and often initiating the verbal contests, as when she asks Dr Middleton for a definition of a 'rough truth' (36). Laetitia Dale's definition, 'caricature', which takes the palm in the definition contest, could be applied to Mrs Mountstuart's own famous sayings:

Her word sprang out of her. She looked at you, and forth it came: and it stuck to you, as nothing laboured or literary could have adhered. Her saying of Laetitia Dale: 'Here she comes, with a romantic tale on her eyelashes,' was a portrait of Laetita. And that of Vernon Whitford: 'He is a Phoebus Apollo turned fasting friar,' painted the sunken brilliancy of the lean long-walker and scholar at a stroke. (2)

The other verbal fencers at the Hall are judged in relation to Mrs Mountstuart. When juxtaposed with her fresh-minted sayings, the learned quotations of the classical scholars who haunt the Hall seem extremely stale. Having completely misunderstood and grossly misquoted Professor Crooklyn on modern English and German scholarship, she complains when he (rightly) corrects her: 'He pores over a little inexactitude in phrases, and pecks at it like a domestic fowl' (33). Dr Middleton's habit of quoting the Classics is so ingrained that his daughter actually states what he would have quoted had he been on hand to comment. When discussing 'the world' with Vernon Whitford she says, 'Papa would quote the "mulier formosa"' (from the *Ars Poetica*) (8). Later, when musing on Harry Oxford, now married to Miss Durham, she thinks: 'Papa would call him her Perseus' (10). Vernon Whitford considers that Dr Middleton's 'humour of sententiousness and doctorial stilts is a mask he delights in' (27). This mask shields him from change, anathema to him as to Sir Willoughby. He thus takes up a position exactly opposite to Mrs Mountstuart's: 'Touch the Greeks, and you can nothing new: all has been said' (20). (One is reminded of Casaubon.) Both the old classical allusions, however, and the new but quotable sayings and epigrams exchanged within the Patterne Hall circle define that circle's closure, excluding the world.

Meredith's portrayal of Patterne Hall and its inhabitants seems to draw upon and implicitly remind the reader of more than one set of literary motifs and contexts. The country house and its grounds, the setting for clever dialogues between a wide variety of characters, including a bibulous cleric and sundry scholars, are suggestive of the locations of the novels of Peacock, Meredith's father-in-law. A Peacockian ivory tower, the Hall is also its dandiacal owner's salon, and the *haut ton* manners and conversation cultivated by Sir Willoughby and his circle are reminiscent of Disraeli's and Bulwer's high-society novels, brilliantly parodied in Carlyle's *Sartor Resartus* (III.10) and Dickens's *Bleak House* (12)[7]. The Carlylean clothes theme in *The Egoist* also suggests similarities between Sir Willoughby and the egoistical Regency dandy. He is fastidious in his tastes, being habitually concerned about the cut, or *pattern*, of his clothes, preferring riding to walking, engaging in exchanges of epigrams, and addressing Clara and Laetitia in 'unmanlike' and 'artificial' speech (6, 31). Clara has a liking for poetry and sometimes quotes 'the stuff' in defiance of Sir Willoughby's 'pursed mouth and pained murmur: "I am no poet"' (6). Like Mrs Mountstuart, he likes to be quoted rather than to quote, and develops his own 'poetry of the enclosed and fortified bower' (6). As a post-Georgian dandy who has withdrawn from London's clubland and established a country salon for himself, he is disgusted to hear Clara assert that it is our duty to love 'the living world' and add: 'I remember hearing Mr. Whitford say that cynicism is intellectual dandyism without the coxcomb's feathers; and it seems to me that cynics are only happy in making the world as barren to others as they have made it for themselves' (7). Clara's realisation that the life Sir Willoughby offers her within his enclosed bower is barren or dead, cold or stone-like, dark or cave-like, is remarkably similar to Dorothea's discovery of her husband's true nature in *Middlemarch*. Earlier in the chapter just quoted, Clara despairs at the thought of a lifetime 'fixed at the mouth of a mine', having to 'descend it daily, and not to discover great opulence below; on the contrary, to be chilled in subterranean sunlessness, without any substantial quality that she could grasp, only the mystery of inefficient tallow-light in those caverns of the complacent talking man'. Later, convinced that 'this immoveable stone-man' will not release her, she conceives the state of marriage with him 'as that of a woman tied not to a man of heart, but to an obelisk lettered all over with hieroglyphics, and everlastingly hearing him expound them, relishingly renewing his lectures on them' (10).

Because one senses a tradition of other Egoists, other complacent talking men, behind Sir Willoughby, Clara's response to this particular obelisk lettered all over with hieroglyphics implies an indictment of generations of upper-class English males, dandiacal without and stone-like within. Meredith conveys this sense of a tradition through implicit parallels to and muted echoes of literary conventions and motifs rather than through specific quotations and references. Similarly, when he echoes a specific text, Pope's *The Rape of the Lock* (the poem which Beardsley was later to interpret as a study of proto-dandies simpering in salon-like interiors), his allusiveness could be described as an aspect of his 'poetry', that stylised intensification of descriptive narrative which subordinates the demands of plot to the imaginative portrayal of character and scene in the novel.

Meredith's description of Sir Willoughby admiring Clara's hair is less a quotation from the *Rape* than an embellishment on Pope:

> [He] doated on her cheek, her ear, and the softly dusky nape of her neck, where this way and that the little lighter-coloured irreclaimable curls running truant from the comb and knot – curls, half-curls, root-curls, vine-ringlets, wedding-rings, fledgeling feathers, tufts of down, blown wisps – waved or fell, waved over or up or involutedly, or strayed, loose and downward, in the form of small siken paws, hardly any of them much thicker than a crayon shading, cunninger than long round locks of gold to trick the heart. (9)

Similarly, Meredith's handling of the imps which haunt Sir Willoughby, scaled down, mock-heroic Eumenides in the House of Patterne, is reminiscent of Pope's treatment of the 'light militia of the lower sky' (*Rape*, I.42). Other spirits which inhabit the Hall are more obviously reminiscent of the poem. When De Craye comes upon Clara by the lake he sees her as a 'union of princess and sylph' (42). In the chapter which follows, Meredith adopts a mock-Popean style, unmistakably based upon the *Rape*, when describing Clara's challenge to Sir Willoughby concerning his proposal to Laetitia:

> Unhappily all the Delicacies (a doughty battalion for the defence of ladies until they enter into difficulties and are shorn of them at a blow, bare as dairymaids), all the body-guard of a young gentlewoman, the drawing-room sylphides, which bear her train, which wreathe her hair, which modulate her voice and tone her complexion, which are arrows and shield to awe the creature man, forebade her utterance of what she felt, on pain of instant fulfilment of their oft-repeated threat of late to leave her to the last remnant of a protecting sprite. She could not, as in a dear melodrama, from the aim of a pointed finger denounce him, on the testimony of her instincts, false of speech, false in deed. (43)

Her melodramatic outburst when she rides into a ford shouting 'Marriage!', during a brief spell of freedom beyond the bounds of the Hall (22), has no place in the claustrophobic, convention-bound indoor life of the house, in which emotion is repressed and can be conveyed only in some formal, indirect way. (Similarly, Sir Willoughby shouts the 'theatric call "Fooled!"', one of the 'stage-cries which are cries of nature', on a rainy road (29), but once inside the Hall suppresses such outbursts with an iron will.) The objective correlatives of emotion within such narrow bounds need be no weightier than Pope's wigs, sword-knots, playing cards, puffs, powders and patches. (The breaking of the porcelain vase, reminiscent of the flawed china jar in the *Rape* (II.106)[8], is a case in point.) Indeed, Pope would have understood Meredith's comments on the Book of Egoism in his Prelude to *The Egoist*, being himself a master of compression and the use of the trope of synecdoche:[9]

> Wise men are strong in their opinion that we should encourage the Comic Spirit, who is, after all, our own offspring, to relieve the Book. Comedy, they say, is the true diversion, as it is likewise the key of the great Book, the music of the Book. They tell us how it condenses whole sections of the Book in a sentence, volumes in a character; so that a fair part of a book outstripping thousands of leagues when unrolled, may be compassed in one comic sitting.

One's sense of the pressure of earlier literary treatments of Meredith's themes, of conventions and motifs 'behind' *The Egoist*, is a response to a kind of playful allusiveness which 'condenses' and adapts, and which cannot easily be pinned down.

III

Within the bower of Patterne Hall, then, Clara is hemmed in by her bodyguard of drawing-room sylphides and protecting sprites, and Sir Willoughby, haunted by imps, tries to keep his sense of equilibrium by clothing himself and others in the conventions of dress and language of his own salon. Clara's escape, however, is prompted by events which occur out of doors, where the clothing of social conventions is shed to reveal primitive man beneath. Moving outside the Hall, I want to concentrate upon Meredith's handling of the famous cherry-tree incident (11–12). This cultivated tree, growing in the trim park, represents the half-way point between Patterne Hall, the bower in which Clara is trapped, and the world of freedom beyond the park. Critics have associated the double-blossom cherry-tree with the escape motif in the novel, albeit only implicitly, through the parallels between Meredith's plot of betrothals and jiltings and the story of the famous Willow Pattern, echoed in Sir Willoughby's name and explicitly mentioned in relation to jilting in the novel (34). Robert Mayo summarised the generally agreed outline of the Willow story in the first detailed discussion of *The Egoist* and the Willow Pattern:

> The rich and influential mandarin who inhabited the stately mansion depicted on the right in the design was a widower possessed of a lovely daughter named Koong-see. He intended to marry his daughter to a wealthy suitor of high degree, but the maiden opposed her parent's wish. She had chosen for her lover a poor and honorable man serving as her father's secret-ary and had exchanged vows with him in clandestine meetings under the blossoming trees of the Willow Pattern. Suspecting his daughter's defection, the mandarin imprisoned her in a pavilion in his garden, and commanded her to marry the husband of his choice when the peach tree should be in blossom. Here Koong-see pined for her freedom, and prayed that she might find release. Her chosen lover found means to communicate with her, invaded her prison, and carried her off, while her father feted the promised bridegroom in the banquet hall. The lovers were hotly pursued by the mandarin (in some versions by Ta-jin, the rejected suitor), but they escaped over the Willow bridge. After further adventures the gods turned them into birds in token of their fidelity.[10]

Mayo concludes his discussion with the assertion that, although the Willow legend provided Meredith with a rough outline for his novel, 'the resemblance between the two stories is too much obscured by indirectness to heighten appreciably our feeling of *pattern* or *form* in the narrative, or to serve effectively as an ironic augury of Sir Willoughby's fate', and that the device is more an '*accessory*' than anything else (Mayo, pp. 77–8). Writ-ing on the porcelain-pattern leitmotif in the novel, Daniel

Schwarz questioned Mayo's conclusions and claimed that 'the nexus between romantic legend and dramatic action is not an elaborate ornament but the foundation of the . . . most important pattern of figurative language' of a novel in which Sir Willoughby attempts to 'impose his designs on others, while the comic imps are shaping a pattern of disappointment and reversal for him'.[11] Schwarz was right to emphasise the importance of this leitmotif. The problem, however, of the status of the close parallels between the Willow story and *The Egoist* has not been fully explored. These parallels include the obvious similarity between the functions of the peach-blossom in the story and the cherry-blossom in the novel. Mayo is tentative on the matter, saying that in the cherry-tree 'we may find a reflection of the lush floral background of the Willow love story' (Mayo, p. 74). It could be argued that Meredith simply offered his reader another of his vague hints concerning the parallels by making a *cherry*-tree a central symbol in the novel, a peach-tree being too close to the Willow original. The cherry-tree in the novel, however, is important in its own right, and has some of the special qualities with which Meredith endows it in his poetry. Moreover, I believe another crucial parallel is adumbrated in the cherry-tree scenes: that between the central characters in *The Egoist* and the mythology pertaining to Diana of the Wood.

Early in the novel, the central characters are associated in an apparently casual and unconnected way with various figures from Roman mythology, all of whom are themselves associated with trees or forest glades, by means of shorthand notations. Vernon Whitford likens Clara to 'the Mountain Echo' (4). On the other hand, Sir Willoughby, Narcissus to Clara's Echo, is enraptured by the Clara whose 'reception of his caress' is cold, 'statue-like, Dian-like' (7). Her own father tells Sir Willoughby that the 'nymph of the woods is in her' (20). Fittingly, Sir Willoughby calls Laetitia Dale 'his Egeria' (4, 34), meaning his tutelary goddess, his female adviser. Egeria was a lesser deity associated with myths and rituals of Diana-worship. Sir James Frazer's monumental study of magic and religion, *The Golden Bough* (1890–1915) grew out of his investigation of the mythology surrounding Diana of the Wood, goddess of fertility in general and of childbirth in particular, at Nemi in Italy, and a brief summary of this mythology, based on Frazer, can serve as a guide to the parallels which Meredith hints at in *The Egoist*.

Within Diana's sanctuary at Nemi there grew a tree of which no branch might be broken, except by a runaway slave. If such a slave succeeded in plucking a bough of the tree he was entitled to fight the priest at Nemi in single combat, and if he killed the priest he assumed his rule over the sanctuary with the title of King of the Wood. The ancients believed that the branch of this tree was the Golden Bough which Aeneas plucked before attempting his journey to the underworld. Diana, the presiding goddess, also had the title of Vesta, which suggests that a holy fire was perpetually maintained in the sanctuary. Egeria was one of two lesser divinities who shared the sanctuary, a nymph of clear water in a stream from which the Vestals fetched water with which to wash the temple of Vesta. According to Plutarch, the Romans believed that Egeria was a Dryad, a nymph of the oak who presided over every green oak grove.

Frazer drew on sources which were familiar to Meredith (some of which he cites in *The Egoist*), including the *Aeneid* and the *Metamorphoses*, Catullus and Plutarch. Although it would probably not have been recognised by many Victorian readers, the mythology of Diana of the Wood would have been familiar to such educated classicists as Meredith, creator of Dr Middleton and Vernon Whitford, and Macaulay, whose passing reference to the source of the army at the battle of Lake Regillus in the *Lays of Ancient Rome* (1842) Frazer adopted as his title-page motto:

> . . . the still glassy lake that sleeps
>   Beneath Aricia's trees –
> Those trees in whose dim shadow
>   The ghastly priest doth reign,
> The priest who slew the slayer
>   And shall himself be slain.
>   ('Battle of the Lake Regillus', X)

Meredith's apparently casual references to Diana and Egeria prove to be related to important symbolism associated with the cherry-tree which grows in the park at Patterne Hall. Soon after her arrival at the Hall, Clara receives a bunch of wild flowers from the devoted Crossjay (9). The bouquet, obviously arranged by Laetitia Dale, includes a branch bearing thick white blossom. Dr Middleton explains to his daughter that this is a 'gardener's improvement on the Vestal of the forest, the wild cherry'. The

classicist justifies the title of the 'Vestal of civilization' for the tree
by explaining that the gardener has 'improved away the fruit' in
cultivating the double blossom. Sir Willoughby is amused to see
that Crossjay has despoiled the 'Holy Tree' worshipped by
Vernon Whitford. When Sir Willoughby says that he would like
to test the complexions of Laetitia and Clara by placing them
under the tree together, Dr Middleton exclaims that he is 'invest-
ing the hamadryad with novel and terrible functions'. The
contiguity of the Diana and Egeria figures and references to the
Vestal and hamadryad suggests an association between Diana
and white cherry-blossom which is to be developed in subsequent chapters.

In chapter 11 of *The Egoist*, 'The Double-Blossom Wild
Cherry-Tree', Sir Willoughby conducts Clara to a group of
laurels, 'there to revel in her soft confusion'. A 'devouring male
Egoist', his primitive ancestry shows itself in the garden, where
he is no longer dandiacal in manner. Clara has to deal with him
as an 'original savage': 'She was required to play incessantly on
the first reclaiming chord which led our ancestral satyr to the
measures of the dance.' She has to be 'cloistral'. Sir Willoughby
delights in her maidenly (Dian-like) resistance to his advances,
for her modesty suggests that he is her first lover and thus can
'own' her completely. Meredith, however, spells out a lesson
which she is soon to learn: 'The capaciously strong in soul
among women will ultimately detect an infinite grossness in the
demand for purity infinite, spotless bloom.' This last metaphor
anticipates the symbolism which is developed later in the chapter. Clara nearly stumbles upon Crossjay as she escapes from Sir
Willoughby, and is directed by the boy to the spot where Vernon
lies asleep: under the Holy Tree, the blooming cherry. Bending
over Vernon to discover the title of the book he was reading when
he fell asleep, Clara immediately, and still with a bent head,

turned her face to where the load of virginal blossom, whiter
than summer-cloud on the sky, showered and drooped and
clustered so thick as to claim colour and seem, like higher
Alpine snows in noon-sunlight, a flush of white. From deep to
deeper heavens of white, her eyes perched and soared. Wonder
lived in her. Happiness in the beauty of the tree pressed to
supplant it, and was more mortal and narrower. Reflection
came, contracting her vision and weighing her to earth. Her

reflection was: 'He must be good who loves to lie and sleep beneath the branches of this tree!' . . . The reflection took root. 'He must be good . . . !' That reflection vowed to endure. Poor by comparison with what it displaced, it presented itself to her as conferring something on him, and she would not have had it absent though it robbed her.

The downward turn in the middle of this crucial paragraph marks a descent from the ideal to the real, from heavens of white to earth, from soaring to rooting. And what takes root will endure. As she reflects on this, Clara literally looks down again, and sees that Vernon is now 'dreamily looking up'. She hurries Crossjay away, playing hound to his hare. When the boy looks round, she is walking listlessly, with a hand at her side.

Meredith ends the chapter here and opens chapter 12 with a description of Vernon coming down to earth in a similar manner. As he wakes he realises that the vision of a 'fair head circled in dazzling blossom' is in fact a reality. Pulling himself together, he jumps to his feet, rattles his throat, plants firmness on his brow and, true alpinist that he is, attacks the 'dream-giving earth with tremendous long strides, that his blood might be lively at the throne of understanding'. Crossjay overtakes him and reports that Clara has 'bumped down' on the ground, feeling her side. She denies that she is unwell, however, and walks on with Vernon at a brisk pace, discussing mountaineering and asserting that she can 'plod': 'Anything to be high up!'

The sequence in which these events occur is important. Crossjay has guided Clara away from Sir Willoughby and towards Vernon, who lies underneath the barren Vestal of the forest. Liberated for a time from her role as Sir Willoughby's chaste, cold Diana, Clara has lowered her eyes and thoughts from the heavenly perfection of the blossom to the 'good' Vernon. The emotional strain of all this is indicated by her momentary collapse. Vernon has turned his back on his infertile Holy Tree in order to pursue Clara.[12] The mountains which the couple discuss represent freedom to both. Earlier in the novel, Clara longs for 'five weeks of perfect liberty in the mountains' which would prepare her for the 'day of bells' (7). Clara and Vernon do not, however, see the mountains as merely idealised lofty regions, remote from the real world. Indeed, Clara counters Sir Willoughby's attacks on the world by likening it to mountains, although she stops herself before she says too much: 'The world has faults; glaciers have crevasses, mountains have chasms; but is not the effect of the whole sublime? not to admire the mountain and the glacier because they can be cruel, seems to me . . . And the world is beautiful.' (It is immediately after saying this that Clara quotes Vernon on cynicism as 'intellectual dandyism without the coxcomb's feathers'.)

As when he presents Clara with the bunch of wild flowers, Crossjay is doing more than help the plot along in the cherry-tree episode. He becomes a bond between Clara and Vernon, who are later to be seen walking on the firm earth with the lad between them. In some ways he is a King of the Wood figure, Sir Willoughby's truant and runaway slave who has torn off a bough of the infertile cherry-tree, an act which anticipates the cherry-tree incident in which the spell cast on Vernon is broken. As in the case of the Willow Pattern analogues, however, the parallel is not fully developed. The King of the Wood is savage, and perhaps the violence with which Crossjay has purloined a branch from the tree complements Meredith's portrayal of Patterne Hall as the domain of Sir Willoughby the 'original savage'. Other associations seem more important, however, for Crossjay, a spirited member of the younger generation, represents fertility in the novel. Nature is 'very strong in him' and he has to be 'plucked out of the earth, rank of the soil, like a root' when it is time for his lessons with Vernon (4). He is the root from which future generations will spring. He epitomises the spirit of the woods, haunting the bushes, birds-nesting, falling from trees, and sleeping rough in the open air. A Bacchus figure, his hat is adorned with a 'trailer of ivy in a wreath' by Clara, ivy being associated with the god of fertility and fecundity, the god of trees in general who was especially honoured by fruit-growers (19).

With the aid of Crossjay, Clara briefly escapes from Sir Willoughby's bower to have an intimate glimpse of the man with whom she falls in love. Her 'Flight in Wild Weather' (25) takes her beyond the park, again under the guidance of Crossjay. In the early morning the boy appears from behind a tree, and they walk to the post office to collect a letter from Clara's friend. On their way back they pass the cherry-tree in the park: 'The tree seemed sorrowful in its withering flowers of the colour of trodden snow.' The infertile cherry-blossom fades, whereas the knowledge that Vernon 'must be good' endures. The rain which pours down when the storm breaks, marking Clara's revolt against Sir Willoughby, might be expected to presage that fertility which the fading cherry-blossom lacks. Such an expectation is dashed for the present, however. When Clara is about to board the train which is to transport her to London and the 'world', she sees Horace de Craye drive up. Being afraid that Vernon may have seen him and deduced that he has had something to do with her attempted escape, she returns to the Hall, her love for Vernon confirmed in her own heart.

Clara's later and final flight from Patterne Hall takes her beyond the shores of England to the Alps, with Vernon Whitford, leaving Sir Willoughby to a loveless marriage with Laetitia. We have seen that, to Clara, mountains symbolise the world. It is thus significant that Meredith leaves the couple in the Alps in the closing lines of the novel: 'That was upon the season when two lovers met between the Swiss and Tyrol Alps over the Lake of Constance. Sitting between them the Comic Muse is grave and sisterly. But taking a glance at the others of her late company of actors, she compresses her lips' (50). Hope for the future, potential fertility and growth in the world, lies with them and with Crossjay, yet, typically, Meredith offers no more than vague hints concerning the future.

IV

When compared with the ways in which allusion is used in the earlier novels I have examined, Meredith's handling of the mythology of Diana of the Wood, adumbrated rather than sharply defined as a set of parallels, and his allusiveness in the portrayal of the dandiacal Sir Willoughby's bower, seem to be as hazy as the ending to the novel. Indeed, Meredith's general comment on the 'whole cast' of the work being 'against the modern style' (*Letters*, II, 581) could be applied more specifically to his allusions, for a different set of assumptions concerning their function seems to be operating in the novel. Rather than clarifying parallels and associations, symbols and analogies, for the reader, most of the literary echoes I have discussed are playfully poetic or referentially oblique, and Meredith's elusive style confirms that the novel could have been appreciated only by those Victorian readers for whom he was a 'favourite' according to Margaret Oliphant: 'The author of *The Egoist* holds an exceptional position in literature. He is not a favourite with the multitude, but if that is any compensation, he is a favourite with people who are supposed to know much better than the multitude.'[13]

8

Mapping the Victorian Age: *Robert Elsmere*

I

Several contemporary reviews of Thomas Hardy's later fiction contain fascinating comparative references to the early works of Mary Ward. Jeannette Gilder left her readers in no doubt about her own critical preferences when she reviewed *Jude the Obscure* in the New York *World* in 1895:

> When I finished the story I opened the windows and let in the fresh air and I turned to my bookshelves and I said: 'Thank God for Kipling and Stevenson, Barrie and Mrs. Humphry Ward. Here are four great writers who have never trailed their talents in the dirt.'[1]

Three years earlier the *Independent* had carried a review of *Tess of the d'Urbervilles* in which Mary Ward's *The History of David Grieve* (1892) and Hardy's novel were said to be 'the two most important works of fiction recently published' and 'the two which will be most read perhaps, and most talked of for some time to come'.[2] This earlier reviewer, however, would no doubt have disagreed with Gilder's views on the cleanliness of Mary Ward's novels. He bemoans the fact that *Tess* and *David Grieve* are 'striking examples' of the trend 'away from the contemplation of wholesome, invigorating scenes and toward noisome ones'.

The most striking feature of both these reviews is the recognition of the 'greatness' or at least 'importance' of Mary Ward's early work. Yet the writer who was considered by some to be as

116

important as Hardy in the 1890s and by others to be the George Eliot of the late Victorian period was relegated to the ranks of the minor after her death in 1922. Fifty years later, as her work is at last being re-assessed, she is regarded as an important minor writer, never approaching George Eliot or Hardy, but recommended reading for the student of Victorian literature and intellectual history. Her novels are often treated as museum pieces, evidence for the historian of ideas rather than living works of literature. *Robert Elsmere* (1888), her most famous work, is more often quoted as a document than analysed as a novel. This is partly because it is not a great novel and, when compared with *The Egoist* and Hardy's later novels, is decidedly old-fashioned in its themes, style and technique. Nevertheless, *Robert Elsmere* is more than a roman à clef of and for its own decade, as I hope an analysis of Mary Ward's use of allusion in the work will demonstrate.

Owen Chadwick asserts that *Robert Elsmere* was 'an intellectual feast, not reading for the common man' (Chadwick, II, 141). The novel certainly reflects Mary Ward's privileged intellectual background, and would have been completely intelligible only to those who had similar backgrounds. As the daughter of Thomas Arnold, Matthew's younger brother, and later as the wife of Humphry Ward, Oxford don, editor of *The English Poets* and arts critic for *The Times*, Mary Ward was always surrounded by books and the writers of books. Her dinner parties, first in Oxford and later in Russell Square and at 'Stocks', hummed with informed conversation on the political, religious and literary issues of the day. Parts of *Robert Elsmere* seem to have been written specifically for her own circle of Oxford acquaintances, particularly some of those in which she based her characters on Oxford originals. This circle was as small, knowledgeable and critical as that for which she wrote her pamphlet, 'Unbelief and Sin: A Protest' (1881), specifically 'addressed to those who attended the Bampton Lecture of Sunday, March 6th'. Biographical source-hunters have delighted in tracing parallels between characters in *Robert Elsmere* and Mary Ward's acquaintances. Although the novel invites such investigation, familiar problems arise at every turn.

The three most important intellectuals in *Robert Elsmere*, Squire Wendover, Henry Grey and Langham, have received most attention from the source-hunters. The Squire has been seen as a portrait of Mark Pattison, that leading runner in the source-of-Edward-Casaubon-stakes.³ The Rev. H. C. Shuttleworth claimed that much of the Squire's 'smart talk' was 'directly borrowed from Pattison's Memoirs'.⁴ In her introduction to the Westmoreland edition of *Robert Elsmere* (1911), Mary Ward disclosed that she was aware that 'those who knew Mark Pattison may have recognised a few of his more obvious traits' in the 'picture of the Squire' (*Writings*, I, xx). Keen to point out that Pattison would not have been the kind of irresponsible and unfeeling landlord she portrayed in the Squire, she added: '"the Rector" suggests the Squire only so far as outward aspects, a few personal traits, and the two main facts of great learning and a general impatience of fools are concerned' (I, xxii). Thus it is difficult to see whether Mary Ward simply used Pattison, whom she admired, as a model, without intending that her readers should notice the resemblance, or hoped that those who knew 'the Rector' would enjoy her treatment of his 'personal traits'.

At first sight Henry Grey seems to be less problematic. *Robert Elsmere* is dedicated to the memory of Mary Ward's two friends, Laura Octavia Mary Lyttelton and Thomas Hill Green. Many of Henry Grey's statements, gospel to his young acolyte, Elsmere, are in fact transcriptions of Green's writings. Mary Ward wrote of the relationship between source and character in her *Writer's Recollections* (1918): 'in the "Grey" of "Robert Elsmere" I tried to reproduce a few of those traits – traits of a great thinker and teacher, who was also one of the simplest, sincerest, and most practical of men – which Oxford will never forget, so long as high culture and noble character are dear to her' (7). The writer did not restrict herself to printed sources in her pious study of Green in the novel. In a letter to Gladstone, dated 17 April 1888, she wrote: '"The parting with the Christian mythology is the rending asunder of bones & marrow", – words which I have put into Grey's mouth, were words of Mr. Green's to me (though this is for yourself alone).'⁵ As in her statement concerning Pattison and the Squire, however, she was keen to emphasise that she reproduced only traits of her original: 'In Henry Grey I was of course thinking of . . . Thomas Hill Green. . . . But the character of Grey is in no sense a portrait of T. H. Green' (*Writings*, I, xli). Again, the would-be source hunter is confronted with the kind of contradictory evidence which is often presented by writers commenting on their own source material.

Langham, the third and last character with Oxford connections, is a complex case, having more than one putative source.
Mary Ward herself stated that Langham was the fruit of her
'long communing with the philosophic charm and the tragic
impotence of Amiel' (*Recollections*, 10). (The novelist published
a translation of Amiel's famous *Journal Intime* three years before
Robert Elsmere appeared.) Stephen Gwynn, however, one of her
contemporary critics, claimed that there was a rival source:
'Oxford of the eighties was more inclined to see in Langham
some reproduction of the Balliol tutor, R. L. Nettleship, a
delicate and subtle intelligence, strangely fenced about by
shyness.'[6] Others have suggested that Mary Ward used her
friend Walter Pater as a model for Langham. As in the cases of
the Squire and Grey, the books which Langham reads and the
ideas he expresses are the best guides to his role in the novel.
Thus, turning from sources to allusions, we find Langham
musing on Sénancour (II, 12) and finding refreshment in Mon-
taigne (II.13). His tendencies towards ennui, scepticism, diffi-
dence and aloofness make him a representative figure who
epitomises one kind of intellectual and emotional reaction
against Establishment ideas and assumptions in mid- and late-
Victorian England. This representative quality is the key to the
novel's contemporary success and lasting interest. Mary Ward's
Oxford friends read parts of *Robert Elsmere* as a kind of *roman à
clef* in which Pattison, Green and Nettleship (Green's editor and
memoirist) played major roles. In order to offer an alternative to
the *roman à clef* emphasis which has dominated criticism of
Robert Elsmere, I want to turn to the question of the wider
readership of the novel and to the use of allusion as a means by
which Mary Ward indicates that the major characters and events
are representative in nature.

Robert Elsmere was certainly an 'intellectual feast', in Chadwick's phrase, for Mary Ward's intellectual peers. That it was
'not reading for the common man', however, is belied by its
prodigious success when it was published. Mary Ward reckoned
that almost a million copies were sold by 1911. The demand for
the many editions published in 1888 was unprecedented. The
novelist tells the story of a lady jumping into her compartment in
a train at Waterloo, having just got hold of a copy in great
demand at a circulating library. 'I've got it – I've got it!', she said

to a friend seeing her off, and 'plunged into her book' as they left the station. (Mary Ward records that she found it 'more amusing to sit still' than to reveal her identity (*Recollections*, 12).) Some American man of letters wrote to her in the year of publication: 'I have seen it in the hands of nursery-maids and of shop-girls behind the counters; of frivolous young women who read every novel that is talked about; of business men, professors, and students' (ibid.). In the United States a copy of *Robert Elsmere* and Gladstone's famous review was given away free with every cake of Balsam Fir soap![7] How, then, did Mary Ward manage to make such an intellectual novel a roaring best-seller?

The author herself recorded that it was the problem of suggesting the argument in such a way that 'both the expert and the popular consciousness may feel its force' that made the writing of the novel a hard grind which lasted for a period of three years (*Recollections*, 12). Her method of solving the problem provides an important clue to the lasting qualities of the novel:

> I had to learn that, having read a great deal, I must as far as possible wipe out the traces of reading. All that could be done was to leave a few sign-posts as firmly planted as one could, so as to recall the real journey to those who already knew it, and for the rest, to trust to the floating interest and passion surrounding a great controversy – the *second* religious battle of the nineteenth century – with which it had seemed to me both in Oxford and in London that the intellectual air was charged. (Ibid.)

Although a long novel, the published version of *Robert Elsmere* was considerably shorter than the bulky typescript. Her deliberate compression of her original material laid her open to Gladstone's main criticism in his review of 1888, concerning the way in which Elsmere's formerly secure faith is rapidly undermined: 'A great creed, with the testimony of eighteen centuries at its back, cannot find an articulate word to say in its defence.'[8] Mary Ward mentioned this point in her introduction to the Westmoreland edition:

> The description of the Squire's influence on Robert, the conversations on Christian evidence, were originally much fuller. But as the human interest of the story gained upon me I began to shorten these sections of the story, until in the third year,

immediately before publication, I desperately reduced them, so far as to give some colour, no doubt, to Mr. Gladstone's reproach, though I cannot but think it exaggerated. (*Writings*, I, xxviii–xxix)

Cutting the scholarly argument in order to focus on the 'human interest' may have been a fault in Gladstone's eyes but was a blessing for the general educated reader. Mary Ward claimed that 'in every generation, while a minority is making or taking part in the intellectual process itself, there is an atmosphere, a diffusion, produced around them, which affects many many thousands who have but little share – but little *conscious* share, at any rate – in the actual process' (*Recollections*, 12). The two kinds of reader for whom she wrote, namely 'the scholar' and 'the educated populace', could both fulfil their side of what I have called the reader-narrator contract by bringing their experience of life in the nineteenth century to the novel as they read. Mary Ward considered that 'all novel-writing is a sort of shorthand'; that each reader, in following a human situation, 'unconsciously supplies a vast amount himself': 'A great deal of the effect is owing to things quite out of the picture given – things in the reader's own mind, first and foremost. The writer is playing on common experience; and mere suggestion is often far more effective than analysis' (ibid.). Thus the orthodox side of the argument at the centre of the novel was really supplied by 'the whole system of things in which the readers of the book lived and moved – the ideas in which they had been brought up, the books they read, the churches in which they worshipped, the sermons to which they listened every week' (*Recollections*, 13). This description of orthodoxy neatly summarises what I earlier described as the 'shared culture' to which many allusions in Victorian fiction are a literary signpost. Robert Elsmere is portrayed as a representative of his age, rather than of his decade, and the most impressive parts of the novel are those in which he moves from one phase of development to another, rapidly covering the kind of ground traversed by several generations of Victorians. As she thus mapped the age, Mary Ward used allusion both as a shorthand and as a means of signposting. By attending to allusion in the novel, the modern reader can understand more of the 'whole system of things' in which the book's characters and its first readers lived and moved.

II

The different locations in which Robert Elsmere is portrayed are more than mere backdrops, for the spirit of place in each location suggests parallels between his development and that of nineteenth-century culture. Allusions complement this use of location, marking the various stages in his career. He moves from the Wordsworthian hills of Westmoreland to Murewell rectory in Surrey, where he works as a Kingsleyesque muscular Christian. After the crisis at Murewell he holidays in the Switzerland of Sénancour, returning to London, where he lives and teaches in the spirit of Arnold and Clough.

The novel opens in the Westmoreland of Catherine Leyburn, Elsmere's future wife. Catherine is reminiscent of Dorothea Brooke in many ways, being ardently pious in her reading of the Bible, Thomas à Kempis, Herbert, Jeremy Taylor and Keble (I.1,7). But Catherine is more old-fashioned and inflexible than Dorothea, being born fifty years after her and undergoing no change in the way that George Eliot's heroine does. The old Long Whindale which she loves has undergone changes in recent years. The local vicar and his wife, the Rev. and Mrs Thornburgh, are strongly reminiscent of Jane Austen's Mr and Mrs Bennet, and thus would seem anachronistic in the towns and cities of the 1880s, the decade in which the novel is set.[9] Yet in Westmoreland they are regarded as modern incomers, and the new church, vicarage and schoolhouse look glaringly modern to the local inhabitants (I.2). Vague impressions of dangerous changes in the outside world filter through to Long Whindale, so that Mrs Seaton can assert that the Oxford authorities are now mainly occupied in poisoning the young men's minds 'by free-thinking opinions' (1.3). These changes are, however, merely hints of what is to come later in the novel. In the first book, 'Westmoreland', Elsmere and Catherine come together in changeless scenery which they both love, the scenery of Wordsworth.

The poet seems to haunt Long Whindale. The story of poor Mary Backhouse is balladic, Wordsworthian in flavour (I.10). The face of Catherine's late father is said to have been 'not unlike' Wordsworth's face in outline, and to have borne a strong resemblance to Catherine (I.1,2). When Elsmere stands admiring the view, early in the novel, he has a 'well-worn volume' of Wordsworth in his pocket (I.2). Without consulting it he recites 'It is a beauteous evening, calm and free' under his breath, and his thoughts flit from the 'nun/Breathless with adoration' to Catherine, of whom he has just heard but has yet to meet. When they do meet he finds her 'a spirit, but a woman too '[sic] (I.3),[10] and discovers that she knows her Wordsworth by heart. These early Wordsworth allusions prepare the ground for a crucial episode in the first book, during which Elsmere and Catherine fall in love.

On a walk over the hills with the vicar and the Leyburn sisters, Elsmere argues with Catherine in a friendly way over whether she should take his mackintosh during a heavy downpour of rain. She submits: 'He put the mackintosh round her, thinking, bold man, as she turned her rosy rain-dewed face to him, of Wordsworth's "Louisa", and the poet's cry of longing' (I.7). Having already established that Elsmere knows his Wordsworth and looks at the hills through his eyes, Mary Ward now shows him seeing Catherine as Wordsworth saw 'Louisa' after 'Accompanying Her on a Mountain Excursion':

> She loves her fire, her cottage-home;
> Yet o'er the moorland will she roam
> In weather rough and bleak;
> And, when against the wind she strains,
> Oh! might I kiss the mountain rains
> That sparkle on her cheek. ('Louisa', 13–18)

As they walk on he tells her that he was reading 'Laodamia' the previous day and quotes 'line after line, lingering over the cadences'. Significantly, it is through quoting this poem that Elsmere comes to know Catherine more intimately, for the work has special associations for her:

'It was my father's favourite of all,' she said, in the low vibrating voice of memory. 'He said the last verse to me the day before he died.'

Robert recalled it –

> 'Yet tears to human suffering are due,
> And mortal hopes defeated and o'erthrown
> Are mourned by man, and not by man alone
> As fondly we believe.' [Cf. 'Laodamia', 164-7]

When Elsmere and Catherine recite Wordsworth's poetry they are perpetuating the practice of their parents' generation. The Victorian Wordsworth was on the lips of educated men and women throughout the careers of Tennyson, Browning and Arnold, and a handful of his best known poems were part of that small stock of literary works through which Catherine and her father, and Catherine and Elsmere, could share their 'common experience', in Mary Ward's phrase.

Having established a sense of intimacy through quotation, Mary Ward spoils the effect somewhat by introducing another marked quotation, this time from Herbert, through which Elsmere again expresses his sympathy with Catherine as she thinks of her dead father. More important is the description of the couple crossing a swollen river on stepping-stones:

He leaped on the first and held out his hand to her. When they started she would have refused his help with scorn. Now, after a moment's hesitation she yielded, and he felt her dear weight on him as he guided her carefully from stone to stone. In reality it is both difficult and risky to be helped over stepping-stones. You had much better manage for yourself; and half way through Catherine had a mind to tell him so. But the words died on her lips which smiled instead . . . . he could have vowed that anything so lovely as that delicately cut, gravely smiling face, swaying above the rushing brown water, was never seen in Westmoreland wilds before.

As it stands, the scene is moving in its simplicity. When read with Catherine's and Elsmere's knowledge of Wordsworth in mind it is suggestive of timeless, pastoral love, being based upon Wordsworth's second sonnet on 'The Stepping-Stones' (X), in his 'River Duddon' series:

> A sweet confusion checks the Shepherd-lass;
> Blushing she eyes the dizzy flood askance;
> To stop ashamed – too timid to advance;
> She ventures once again – another pause! . . .
>
>   . . . the thrilling touch
> Both feel, when he renews the wished-for aid.
>   (3-6, 9-10)

The stepping-stones passage in *Robert Elsmere* is not merely a borrowing from an unacknowledged Wordsworthian source. Following the allusions to Wordsworth and his poetry quoted above, this parallel passage reads as a kind of narrative 'reference' to the Duddon sonnet.

The cumulative effect of the descriptions of nature at its freshest and purest, and of the Wordsworth allusions, suggestive of what Keats called 'the holiness of the Heart's affections', is shattered when Mrs Thornburgh tactlessly alerts the proud, virginal Catherine to the fact that Elsmere's attraction to her has been noticed. She submits to Elsmere, however, after a long period of inner struggle between Duty and Love, and becomes his wife. From the time she leaves Westmoreland, when Elsmere takes over his Surrey rectory, both husband and wife think of this Wordsworth country with nostalgia. It is an idealised countryside for which both long, like other Victorians before them.

Early in their marriage, Elsmere and Catherine settle down to a life together in which both are secure in the knowledge that their beliefs and aspirations, and their mutual love and respect, have stabilised. The grand chords of the 'Westmoreland' chapters, in which each partner explores his or her innermost self as if in the presence of Wordsworth, have faded into the background. The tone of the second book, 'Surrey', is more restrained, reflecting the more workaday aspects of life. Catherine is fulfilled in her roles of wife and helpmate, and later as mother. At this stage Elsmere is a balanced figure. Within the Anglican church, itself the *via media*, he has a central stance as a Broad Churchman. For example, he takes the middle ground between the puritanical Catherine and the High Church ritualist, Newcome (II. 11, 12). In his day-to-day existence he balances heart and head, body and mind, in the *mens sana* spirit of the muscular Christian: active parish work is combined with study in Squire Wendover's library. Mary Ward hints at Elsmere's similarity to Charles Kingsley early in the novel, when he makes a Christian case for pursuing the life of an artist 'very much as Kingsley would have argued it' (I.6). At this time Catherine learns much about 'modern character' by seeing how he is preparing himself for his living in Surrey: 'reading up the history, geology, and botany of the Weald and its neighbourhood, plunging into reports of agricultural commissions, or spending his quick brain on village sanitation.' This passage precedes the reference to Kingsley by only a few paragraphs and is strikingly close to accounts of Kingsley's own work at Eversley, Hampshire, and particularly to the *Letters and Memories*, edited by his wife and published in 1877.

To the many readers of *Robert Elsmere* who were familiar with Kingsley's writings and biography, Elsmere's work and recreation at Murewell must have seemed unmistakably similar to the famous parson's way of life. For example, when Langham visits the Elsmeres at Murewell he is intrigued by the study:

> Then they plunged into the study, he and Robert, and smoked their fill. The study was an astonishing medley. Books, natural history specimens, a half-written sermon, fishing-rods, cricket-bats, a huge medicine cupboard – all the main elements of Elsmere's new existence were represented there. In the drawing-room with his wife and his sister-in-law he had been as much of a boy as ever; here clearly he was a man, very much in earnest. What about? What did it all come to? . . . Langham approached the subject with his usual scepticism. (II.12)

Throughout *Robert Elsmere*, Mary Ward gives detailed descriptions of houses and rooms within houses as outward and visible signs of the nature of their occupants. This description of Elsmere's study is remarkably close to that of Kingsley's study in the *Letters and Memories* (I.10). Kingsley seems to be speaking through Elsmere when the latter tells Langham that 'dirt and drains' are the 'foundations of a sound religion' (II.12). Elsmere's pride in his Workmen's Institute, and his passion for natural history, are also reminiscent of Kingsley's energetic activities in the field and lecture hall (II.13).

Confirmation of these parallels comes in the form of an explicit reference to Elsmere's precursor: 'He talked of fishing as Kingsley might have talked of it, and, indeed, with constant quotations from Kingsley' (II.13).[11] Elsmere, however, is no more a portrait of Kingsley than the Squire is a portrait of that hidden source, Pattison. Rather, Mary Ward refers to Kingsley as a famous representative figure of the mid-Victorian era. It is significant that Walter Houghton often turns to Kingsley's writings and biography in order to illustrate aspects of the

'Victorian Frame of Mind'. Although idiosyncratic in many ways, his earnestness, his nervous energy, and his muscular Christianity are traits shared by many of his generation. Elsmere, himself a representative figure in the novel, is thus shown to pass through a phase in his own life which can be closely compared with a phase in the life of the century. The older Squire Wendover, owner of neighbouring Murewell Hall, dismisses what he sees as 'enthusiasm' with a sneer: 'One may make it a maxim of general experience, and take it as fitting all the fools with a mission who have teased our generation – all your Kingsleys, and Maurices, and Ruskins – every one bent upon making any sort of aimless commotion, which may serve him both as an investment for the next world, and an advertisement for this' (II.17). Although the Squire is speaking to a group of people, this biting comment is aimed mainly at Elsmere, who, with the zeal of a Kingsley in matters of sanitary reform, has taken the Squire to task for allowing his houses at Mile End to fall into a scandalous state. Unlike Kingsley, whose faith was untroubled by Darwin, for example, Elsmere's faith is soon shattered. Fittingly, it is his research in the library at the Hall and his reading of the Squire's own sceptical writings that undermine the fabric of his belief and thus of the balanced and well ordered family life he enjoys with Catherine at the rectory.

Mary Ward is most impressive in her use of a house and its interior when she describes Murewell Hall and its library. English cultural history can be read in the house, its contents and its garden. Sidney visited the house, Elizabeth stayed there twice, and Waller left a copy of verses in the library (II.11). Lord Clarendon wrote part of his History in the garden, itself partly Evelyn's work. The Hall, a 'majestic relic of a vanished England', contains splendid art treasures dating from the Renaissance (II.14). But to Elsmere and his visitor, Langham, whom he shows round, the library is by far the most impressive part of the house. The main room of the library contains the oldest and rarest volumes in the large collection, including copies of works by famous sixteenth- and seventeenth-century English writers which were presented to the Squire's ancestors, and books which belonged to Addison, Sir William Temple, Swift and Horace Walpole. Like the rest of the house, this part of the collection grew slowly over the centuries, as if organically: 'only a small proportion of these precious things represented conscious and deliberate acquisition', for most of them 'drifted thither one by one, carried there by the tide of English letters as to a warm and natural resting-place'.

The 'working parts' of the Squire's library are quite different and are stored in a business-like way in rooms leading off the large 'ornamental sensational part of the library', as Elsmere calls it. Here the book titles can be read as what Mary Ward calls a 'chart' of the Squire's 'intellectual history'. The shelves are filled with books collected at Oxford during the Tractarian Movement, and with books acquired during ten years of study in Germany which represent those 'forces of an epoch' which were to influence the mind of Europe for three generations. Although attracted to the old library, instinct with the spirit of the old Hall, Elsmere is most interested in the Squire's working library, where the young rector has his own corner in which to work on a historical study of the making of France, while the Squire is away. When Elsmere outlines the early stages of his research on the history of Europe, Langham the Oxford tutor quickly puts his finger on the problem which his amateur friend will have to tackle:

> To my mind, it makes almost the chief interest of history. It is just this. History depends on *testimony*. What is the nature and the value of testimony at given times? In other words, did the man of the third century understand, or report, or interpret facts in the same way as the man of the sixteenth or the nineteenth?

The problem of testimony is summarised here for both Elsmere and the reader. When Elsmere comments 'reflectively' that it is indeed 'enormously important', Langham points out that 'the whole of orthodox Christianity is in it'. Elsmere is soon to examine the problem in relation to his own research and to biblical hermeneutics, proving to himself that belief in miracles, a corner-stone of orthodox Christianity, rests upon the doubtful testimony of those who wrote the biblical account of Jesus's ministry. He thus enters another phase of his intellectual development which others, influenced by German criticism, have already passed through. Langham raises the problem of testimony in the room in which the Squire has spent years writing a massive history of testimony and shorter works, including *The Idols of the Market-place*, which is to rock Elsmere's faith (III.20). The urgency of Elsmere's reading and thinking suggests the sense of urgency of the period of rapid change in intellectual history in the middle years of the nineteenth century. The Squire's own work in his library belongs to this period. Thus the references to the Squire's copies of the works of Niebuhr, Strauss, Baur, Ewald, and others, are examples of what Mary Ward called 'sign-posts', placed 'so as to recall the real journey to those who already knew it'. Similarly, Langham's comments on testimony serve as 'shorthand'. In the chapters which follow, Elsmere's reading and his discussions with the Squire lead to a crisis of faith which in turn forces him to give up his living. He can no longer fulfil the role of a Kingsley in the parish which he and his wife have come to love.

During the period of transition from faith to doubt, described in the third book, 'The Squire', Elsmere comes to envy his wife's faith. When he reads her passages from Augustine's *Confessions*, her favourite book, he is made acutely aware of 'that intense spiritual life of Catherine's which in its wonderful self-containedness and strength was always a marvel, sometimes a reproach, to him' (III.19). On returning from a walk, during which he has mulled over questions of faith, he catches sight of 'the tower and chancel window of the little church':

> In an instant he had a vision of early summer mornings – dewy, perfumed, silent, save for the birds, and all the soft stir of rural birth and growth, of a chancel fragrant with many flowers, of a distant church with scattered figures, of the kneeling form of his wife close beside him, himself bending over her, the sacrament of the Lord's death in his hand. The emotion, the intensity, the absolute self-surrender of innumerable such moments in the past – moments of a common faith, a common self-abasement – came flooding back upon him. With a movement of joy and penitence he threw himself at the feet of Catherine's Master and his own: '*Fix there thy resting-place, my soul!*' [Augustine]

Anglican communion in a rural church is part of that 'common experience', the 'whole system of things in which the readers of the book lived and moved' and which Elsmere has to reject. He is wavering at this stage, tempted to suppress his doubts and give himself over to the 'whole system' of orthodoxy, thus not sacrificing public approval, the love and respect of his wife, and the right to administer the sacraments in an English parish church. The emotional and intellectual cosiness of orthodoxy, particularly in such a setting, is extremely attractive, and although Elsmere's grasp of what he is to see as the truth proves stronger than his longing for the old security which his living represents, he often looks back with regret. When Catherine is still asking him to share his problems with her, he asks her to read him 'that Duddon sonnet' she used to read aloud during their courtship in Westmoreland (III.25). He is soothed by the lines:

'Enough, if something from our hand have power
To live and move, and serve the future hour,
And if, as towards the silent tomb we go,
Through love, through hope, and faith's transcendent dower,
We feel that we are greater than we know.'
(Cf. 'The River Duddon', XXXIV)

Like his nostalgic memories of services in his country church, Elsmere's yearning for the old Westmoreland days is a symptom of nervous fatigue. In fact he knows that he will never again be the young man who helped Catherine over the stepping-stones. The sense of oneness with man and nature which Wordsworth and the hills nurtured in him, and the balanced life of a busy country parson, are to give way to anxiety and uncertainty, and to a restless life in a modern, urban environment.

The 'Crisis' of the fourth book occurs in the wooded countryside which Elsmere and Catherine love, near the rectory. It seems to Elsmere that he is going through the 'old fierce temptation of Bunyan's': 'To sell and part with this most blessed Christ; to exchange Him for the things of life, for anything!' (IV.26; *Grace Abounding*, 132-5). He goes through a 'desperate catechism of himself', asking whether he believes in '*the Man-God*, the Word from Eternity', and waiting for the answer in the knowledge that this is 'the crisis of his history'. The answer soon comes: 'Every human soul in which the voice of God makes itself felt, enjoys, equally with Jesus of Nazareth, the divine sonship, and "*miracles do not happen!*"' The italicised words are from the last sentence in the 1883 preface to *Literature & Dogma*, by Mary

Ward's beloved 'Uncle Matt': 'But our popular religion at present conceives the birth, ministry, and death of Christ, as altogether steeped in prodigy, brimful of miracle; – *and miracles do not happen.*' This is the most important quotation in the novel, expressing the central idea which forces the crisis in Elsmere's life. He again feels like Bunyan: 'Now was the battle won, and down fell I as a bird that is shot from the top of a tree' (*Grace Abounding*, 140). The lane darkens round him. He walks home mechanically and leans on the gate at the bottom of his garden before going in to see his wife. The scene recalls an earlier episode in happier times, when Elsmere, 'leaning over a gate' in the Westmoreland countryside, realises that he wants Catherine to be his wife (I.6). Mary Ward then quoted Matthew Arnold's 'Resignation' ('Tears/Were in his eyes . . .', cf. 186–8), the poem of 1849 in which Arnold describes the poet who 'leans upon a gate' (144–73). In Westmoreland, Elsmere is associated with the poet Arnold who revered Wordsworth. During and after the Murewell crisis he moves into a later Arnoldian phase.

The Elsmeres' move from Murewell to London is described in a crucial chapter in the fifth book (V.32). The chapter opens with an account of the couple on a foreign holiday, trying to renew their old intimacy and mutual understanding, but failing because of the barrier raised between them by Elsmere's loss of faith. Here again the location is carefully chosen. It is 'Obermann' country, the area of Switzerland in which Sénancour lived and where he wrote the melancholy epistolary novel which Matthew Arnold found so moving, and on which he wrote his two famous poems: 'Stanzas in Memory of the Author of "Obermann", November, 1849' (1852) and 'Obermann Once More, Composed Many Years After the Preceding' (1867). The Elsmeres settle in a hotel at Les Avants, three thousand feet above the eastern shore of Lake Geneva, in an area which is strongly reminiscent of that described in Arnold's 'Stanzas in Memory' (25–36). Mary Ward's marked quotation from 'Obermann Once More' ('the "Valais depths profound"', cf. 347) alert the reader who knows the poem to the parallels between Obermann and Elsmere. In a vision, the shade of Obermann addresses Arnold on the 'immedicable pain'

> 'Which to the wilderness drove out
> Our life, to Alpine snow,

> And palsied all our word with doubt,
> And all our work with woe –
>
> 'What still of strength is left, employ
> That end to help attain:
> *One common wave of thought and joy*
> *Lifting mankind again!'*   (316–24)

Elsmere retraces the steps of Arnold who retraced the steps of Sénancour in Switzerland. Again, the Victorians have been here before.

When Catherine and Elsmere return to London, the polarisation of their creeds is marked by her joining the church of a 'narrow Evangelical' and his searching for 'new ways of worship and new forms of love' (V.32). Mary Ward comments that many, like Elsmere, must be 'watching . . . through the darkness for the rising of a new City of God!' The direction which Elsmere himself takes in search of 'New Openings' (Book VI) is indicated in this same transitional chapter (V.32). He stands in Parliament Square admiring the sunset behind the Abbey, recalling the words of a German friend the previous day: 'your venerable Abbey is to me the symbol of a nationality to which the modern world owes obligations it can never repay.' Today Elsmere walks away from the Abbey, that grandest expression of the orthodoxy which Murewell church represented to him, and down the Embankment: 'Carrying the poetry and grandeur of England's past with him, he turned his face eastward to the great new-made London on the other side of St. Paul's, the London of the democracy, of the nineteenth century, and of the future.' Although always tending towards the over-explicit, Mary Ward's handling of location has been more subtle and less obtrusive than this earlier in the novel. Here she overtly comments on the significance of Elsmere's movements where it would have been better to have made the reader do the work.

The church has largely failed in the East End, a 'human wilderness' as Elsmere describes it. As he prepares himself for 'raw and uncomely' work, he takes comfort from the much anthologised and unusually hopeful poem, 'Say Not, the Struggle Naught Availeth', by Clough, that other doubter who exiled himself from the Establishment:

> 'While the tired wave vainly breaking,
>   Seems here no painful inch to gain,

Far back through creeks and inlets making,
    Comes silent, flooding in the main!'   [Cf. 9–12]

From now until the end of his short life, Elsmere inhabits the
spiritual and intellectual world of the Arnolds, the Cloughs and
the Sénancours, rather than that of 'your Kingsleys, and
Maurices, and Ruskins' (II.17).

Elsmere explains his new vision of the future of Christianity in
a lecture to a secularist club in the district in which he works for
London artisans (VI.40). The contrast between Murewell church
and the 'large bare hall, glaringly lit, lined with white brick', in a
long street of warehouses in the East End, highlights the sacrifice
Elsmere has made and the challenge of his task. In order to
justify 'The Claim of Jesus upon Modern Life' he describes the
life of Jesus in simple, moving terms, emphasising that the
reading of the gospels must be based upon '*Experience*' and that
'*Miracles do not happen*'. Mary Ward refers to Arnold only
obliquely, saying that Elsmere restated 'Hume's old argument',
adding to it 'some of the most cogent of those modern arguments
drawn from literature, from history, from the comparative study
of religions and religious evidence, which were not practically at
Hume's disposal, but which are now affecting the popular mind
as Hume's reasoning could never have affected it'. Hume's
chapter, 'Of Miracles', in 'Concerning Human Understanding'
(1748; rpt. 1758), though available to Mary Ward's 'scholar'
reader in a recent (1874–5) edition by her hero, T. H. Green,
and T. H. Grose, was a far less accessible discussion of 'experience' and 'testimony' to her readers from the 'educated populace'
than was Arnold's *Literature & Dogma*. Mary Ward stated that
her uncle 'threw out in detail much of the argument suggested in
"Robert Elsmere"', but that he was a committed practising
member of the Anglican church until the end of his life, and had
little sympathy with people who 'went out' (*Recollections*, 12).
She recognised that, had he lived to read the whole novel, he
could never have had full sympathy with her main theme, that 'a
priest who doubts must depart', and added that she herself had
come to agree with him years later (ibid.). In his lecture, Elsmere
quotes from 'Obermann Once More':

            'Far hence he lies
              In the lorn Syrian town,

And on his grave, with shining eyes,
        The Syrian stars look down.' (173–6)

The previous, unquoted lines in Obermann's address to Arnold
summarise what he and Arnold and Elsmere have lost:

'While we believed, on earth he went,
And open stood his grave.
Men called from chamber, church, and tent;
And Christ was by to save.

Now he is dead!'   (169–73)

Elsmere, however, stresses the positive things which can be
saved from the wreckage, dwelling on the force which Christian
mythology can still have in the modern world: '*He is risen* – in a
wiser reverence and a more reasonable love; risen in new forms
of social help inspired by his memory, called afresh by his
name!' His lecture and the 'Obermann' allusion illustrate both
sides of the 'Gain and Loss' of the final book (VII). Honesty in
the quest for truth and a dedication to 'new forms of social help'
in a new, raw world have been gained at the expense of old
certainties based on Gladstone's 'testimony of eighteen centuries'.

Elsmere's work in his New Brotherhood of Elgood Street
eventually kills him. The novel ends with authorial commentary
on the growth of the Brotherhood after his death which expresses
Mary Ward's empathy with her hero, whose work in London is
not unlike her own in certain respects:

His effort was but a fraction of the effort of the race. In that
effort, and in the Divine force behind it, is our trust, as was his.

'Others, I doubt not, if not we,
The issue of our toils shall see;
And (they forgotten and unknown)
Young children gather as their own –
The harvest that the dead had sown.'
(VII.51; cf. 'Come, Poet, come', 38–42)

Something of the empathy between Mary Ward and her most
famous character was to remain with her until her death, for

these misquoted lines from Clough's 'Come, Poet, come!' were
to be her epitaph, engraved on her tombstone.

III

The first four books of *Robert Elsmere*, covering the Westmoreland and Murewell periods, are more impressive than the last
three, both in what Mary Ward called their 'human interest' and
in the handling of the hero's problems of faith and doubt. In the
first half of the novel, Elsmere is a representative Victorian. In
the second half he is still a representative figure in certain
respects, but has also become Mary Ward's mouthpiece. In both
halves there is a tendency towards over-explicitness, and Mary
Ward's comments on the effect of a novel owing much to 'things
quite out of the picture given – things in the reader's own mind',
are more applicable to George Eliot's fiction than to her own.
Although one senses the writer's hand at work even in the best
episodes in the early books, where Elsmere's development is
suggested through the use of specific locations and complementary allusions, these early books are less marred by heavy-
handedness than are the London books at the end of the novel.
Elsmere's walk away from the Abbey is pointedly described as a
turning away from the old to the new, and his lecture is, of its
very nature, a kind of apologia for both character and writer.

Mary Ward wrote of Charlotte Brontë's *Shirley* in 1917: 'I
wish that Charlotte had not, as she confessed to Mr. Williams,
photographed the three curates from the life. They have the
faults of photography, in its cruder stages. They are not trans-
muted; they remain raw and clumsy.'[12] Interestingly, the same
photography analogy had been applied to her own technique in
Robert Elsmere in a hostile review of 1888, although the force of
the analogy was slightly different:

> Her Westmoreland scenes and her Oxford scenes and her
> London scenes . . . are evidently all taken with much labour
> from the life; some at least of her personages are almost
> labelled and ticketed 'Copy from So-and-so,' and we should
> not be surprised to find that most of the others were equally
> conscientious studies from the model. Unluckily, this is not
> enough; unluckily, it is very often fatally more than enough.

The constant suggestion of something photographed, something *calqué* [traced, copied] upon the actual, is but an irksome thing in a novel.[13]

This critic would have been fairer had he described the novel as a photograph album of the nineteenth century, each book being a new page full of prints of contemporary life. This would have been only slightly unjust to a novel which captures the tone, the atmosphere of different phases of the nineteenth century, and which shows a representative contemporary moving through phases of his own life which resemble these larger movements. Mary Ward uses all the techniques at her disposal, including allusion, to suggest the sense of loss which is central to the experience of the mid- and late Victorians: loss of faith, loss of confidence in received ideas and conventions, loss of individual identity in an urban environment. In mapping the Victorian age and using allusions as signposts along a route which was familiar to many of her readers, Mary Ward was more than a historian of ideas or a writer of tracts for the times, and *Robert Elsmere* is more than a *roman à clef* of and for the 1880s.

9

The Defects of the Real: *The Return of the Native* and *Tess of the d'Urbervilles*

I

Like George Eliot, Thomas Hardy was interested in the relationship between the real and the ideal, and particularly in the way in which fictional characters portrayed in the real world of the nineteenth century can appear to be belittled when they are idealised and compared with greater precursors. Unlike George Eliot, however, he showed signs of uncertainty in his handling of allusion as a means by which to define the relationship between the real and the ideal, and was often as oblique as Meredith in his use of allusion. (The explicitness of Mary Ward's allusions is an aspect of her rather old-fashioned, mid-Victorian style.) My justification for examining two Hardy novels in this chapter is that they share this real/ideal theme and yet illustrate Hardy's problems with the convention of allusion in quite different ways. Whereas too many allusions were crammed into *The Return of the Native*,[1] several very important allusions were deliberately cut out of *Tess of the d'Urbervilles*. A study of the changes Hardy made in the manuscripts and early editions of these novels reveals that he was uncertain whether to make the relationship between his fiction and earlier literary works public, through allusion, or private, a matter of literary sources.

The publication of the *Return* in 1878 is generally regarded as a turning point in Hardy's career as a novelist. The 'cleverness' of the work seems to suggest a new ambition in Hardy, and an awareness of an intelligent readership for whom he could write.

(At least two of his contemporary reviewers complained that in striving to be clever he had failed to entertain his readers.) Modern critics have argued that his many allusions to classical literature, contemporary poetry, and other kinds of adopted texts are symptomatic of tendencies towards self-advertisement in his fiction and the attempted aggrandisement of characters who actually live in an unheroic age. There is sense in this argument, although many of the allusions which have been criticised seem designed to undermine the status of the characters rather than to elevate it. For example, some of the Promethean references suggest that Clym Yeobright is a pathetically limited product of the nineteenth century rather than a would-be superman who never quite convinces. Louis Crompton writes: 'Hardy's use of heroic archetypes is partly serious and partly ironic, his characters appearing at one moment comparable to their heroic models, at other times ludicrously smaller and weaker.'[2] Where Crompton finds liveliness in these constant variations, and richness in the novel's modal syncretism (romance, high tragedy and modern realistic fiction), other readers have found confusion and clutter. One particular parallel text, however, Keats's *Endymion*, is more important in relation to the *Return* than are the majority of isolated allusions in the novel. *Tess of the d'Urbervilles* (1891) is less cluttered than the *Return*. Hardy's deletions in the manuscript and early editions suggest that he may have recognised the dangers of incorporating too many unconnected references to a number of adopted texts in this later novel,[3] and that even references to his most important adopted text, Ovid's *Metamorphoses*, could have been distracting. Yet allusion underlines a central theme in both novels: the vain pursuit of the ideal in a world in which the defects of natural laws' operate upon the 'defects of the real' (*Return*, III.1; *Tess*, 36).

II

The Return of the Native first appeared as a serial in the monthly *Belgravia* magazine between January and December 1878. The first number has no motto under the title heading, whereas each of the three volumes which make up the first book edition, published in November 1878, has an unascribed title-page motto from Keats's *Endymion*:

> 'To sorrow
> I bade good morrow,
> And thought to leave her far away behind;
> But cheerly, cheerly,
> She loves me dearly;
> She is so constant to me, and so kind.
> I would deceive her,
> And so leave her,
> But ah! she is so constant and so kind.'

It is impossible to tell whether Hardy had the motto in mind before January 1878, but decided not to use it in the serial, or whether he chose it later for the first edition of November. The first explanation is tenable, since title-page mottoes which are to be borne in mind throughout a reading of a volume or an entire novel are less effective in a monthly serial version. Even if the second explanation were correct, however, and Hardy first thought of adding the motto not long before November, the allusion could have the effect of alerting the reader who recognises it to the most important parallel text in the *Return*: the text which can be 'read' alongside the novel. Another initial difficulty concerns the context of the motto in the poem (IV.173–81): the fifth stanza of the Indian Maid's 'roundelay', which she sings 'beneath the midmost forest tree'. Sometimes quoted out of context, the song is one of several atypical passages in the fourth book in which Keats breaks away from the rhyming couplet form of the rest of the poem. The stanza may have been chosen by Hardy merely as a convenient way of striking the key-note of a novel in which Sorrow is 'constant' to its central characters. Indeed, the fact that the motto is unascribed could be said to support this view. The contiguity of numerous themes and motifs in the novel and the poem suggests, however, that the motto could not just as well have been chosen from another source which touched on a similar theme.

Hardy's portrayal of Eustacia Vye in the famous 'Queen of Night' chapter in the first book is an extreme example of overstatement, where he piles reference upon reference and association upon association: Olympus, the Fates, the Sphinx, Paganism, *Athalie*, Artemis, Athena, Hera, Hades, Tartarus, Alcin-

ous, Phaeacia, Heaven, Delphi, Héloïse, and Cleopatra (I.7).
Most of these references could have been omitted without undermining their main function: to emphasise Eustacia's pride and
ambition, and her frustration at being an earth-bound prisoner
in Egdon. Read with *Endymion* in mind, however, certain
passages share common associations. The tension between mortality and divinity which Endymion knows in his love for both
Cynthia, the moon-goddess, and the Indian Maid is paralleled in
the opening sentences of the chapter: 'Eustacia Vye was the raw
material of a divinity. On Olympus she would have done well
with a little preparation. She had the passions and instincts
which make a model goddess, that is, those which make not
quite a model woman' (I.7). (The word 'model', incorporated in
the first and later editions, with its hint of artificiality and
self-consciousness, is an improvement on 'faultless' in the
manuscript[4] and the *Belgravia*[5].) Among the list of mythological
allusions, the reference to the Greek Artemis, generally recognised as being identical to the Roman Diana, whose other name
was Cynthia, makes the parallel between Eustacia and Cynthia
more explicit: 'The new moon behind her head, an old helmet
upon it, a diadem of accidental dewdrops round her brow, would
have been adjuncts sufficient to strike the note of Artemis,
Athena, or Hera respectively, with as close an approximation to
the antique as that which passes muster on many respected
canvases.' Her colouring is that of the Indian Maid, the 'stranger
of dark tresses' (IV.462), and, like Cynthia's (I.591f), her face is
described in relation to the sky and clouds: 'To see her hair was
to fancy that a whole winter did not contain darkness enough to
form its shadow: it closed over her forehead like nightfall
extinguishing the western glow. . . . Across the upper part of her
head she wore a thin fillet of black velvet, restraining the
luxuriance of her shady hair, in a way which added much to this
class of majesty by irregularly clouding her forehead.'
    The shading of Eustacia's face is a recurring motif in the novel,
usually associated with the moon. Clym and Eustacia first speak
to each other in the moonlight after the mummers' play, when
Eustacia's face is veiled with ribbons (II.6). She pushes up her
veil when she signs the register at Wildeve's wedding (II.8) and
later veils herself when she joins the country dance with him, by
moonlight (IV.3). This veiling motif is most skilfully developed
during the eclipse sequence, when Clym is enchanted by Eustacia. With sickening dramatic irony, Clym's mother has al-

ready warned him that he is 'blinded' and that it was a 'bad day'
for him when he 'first set eyes on' Eustacia (III.3). The following
evening he walks on to Rainbarrow and lies down, his face
towards the moon: 'His eye travelled over the length and breadth
of that distant country ... till he almost felt himself to be
voyaging bodily through its wild scenes' (III.4). The eclipsed
moon is reminiscent of Eustacia's face, covered with a veil or
clouded by her black hair: 'While he watched the far-removed
landscape a tawny stain grew into being on the lower verge: the
eclipse had begun. This marked a preconcerted moment: for the
remote celestial phenomenon had been pressed into sublunary
service as a lover's signal. Yeobright's mind flew back to earth at
the sight; he arose, shook himself, and listened.' Having greeted
Eustacia as a lover, he examines her face as he has examined that
of the moon: 'Let me look right into your moonlit face, and dwell
on every line and curve in it! Only a few hair-breadths make the
difference between this face and faces I have seen many times
before I knew you; yet what a difference – the difference between
everything and nothing at all.' The fragility of this vision of
beauty is underlined by frequent references to sight and blindness. As the eclipse comes to an end Eustacia laments that their
'time is slipping, slipping, slipping', and they have to part. In the
final paragraph of the chapter the moon/Eustacia analogy is
made explicit. Clym knows that his love for his mother and his
love for Eustacia are incompatible: 'Thus as his sight grew
accustomed to the first blinding halo kindled about him by love
and beauty, Yeobright began to perceive what a strait he was in.'

As he scrutinises the moon and Eustacia's face, Clym is a
latter-day Endymion, seeing his Cynthia in all her splendour for
the first time:

> Methought I lay
> Watching the zenith . . .
> Spreading imaginary pinions wide.
> When, presently, the stars began to glide,
> And faint away, before my eager view.
> At which I sighed that I could not pursue,
> And dropped my vision to the horizon's verge –
> And lo! from opening clouds, I saw emerge
> The loveliest moon, that ever silver'd o'er
> A shell for Neptune's goblet. She did soar
> So passionately bright, my dazzled soul

Commingling with her argent spheres did roll. . . .

To commune with those orbs, once more I raised
My sight right upward; but it was quite dazed
By a bright something, sailing down apace,
Making me quickly veil my eyes and face.   (I.578–603)

Endymion's dazzling by the vision of Cynthia is as sudden as his
later enchantment by her mortal emanation, the Indian Maid
(IV.85f). On Rainbarrow, Eustacia verges on apotheosis, beaut-
iful in Clym's dazzled eyes and craving for higher things than
Egdon can offer. At once a would-be Cynthia and an Indian
Maid, she is a 'model goddess' and 'not quite a model woman'.

When Eustacia insists on hearing about Paris, during the
conversation on the barrow, the reluctant Clym chooses to
describe a 'sunny room in the Louvre' which he considers a
fitting place for her to live in – the Galerie d'Apollon:

Its windows are mainly east; and in the early morning, when
the sun is bright, the whole apartment is in a perfect blaze of
splendour. The rays bristle and dart from the encrustations of
gilding to the magnificent inlaid coffers, from the coffers to the
gold and silver plate, from the plate to the jewels and precious
stones, from these to the enamels, till there is a perfect network
of light which quite dazzles the eye. (III.4)

Cynthia commands Endymion to 'Descend/ . . . Into the sparry
hollows of the world' (II.202–4). Fearfully he moves into the
underworld:

Dark, nor light,
The region; nor bright, nor sombre wholly,
But mingled up; a gleaming melancholy;
A dusky empire and its diadems;
One faint eternal eventide of gems.
Aye, millions sparkled on a vein of gold,
Along whose track the prince quick footsteps told,
With all its lines abrupt and angular . . . .
Chilly and numb
His bosom grew when first he far away
Descried an orbèd diamond, set to fray
Old darkness from his throne.   (II.221–46)

He then moves into 'a marble gallery, passing through / A mimic temple', sees 'a fair shrine' and, 'just beyond, on light tiptoe divine, / A quivered Dian', before which he veils his 'eye' (II.256–63). In this alien place he finds that 'thoughts of self' come on, 'how crude and sore / The journey homeward to habitual self' (275–6). Back on his native heath, as his 'habitual self', Clym is uneasy about recalling his Paris experiences, knowing that what was alien to him is apparently Eustacia's idea of the perfect home. (When Hardy decided to make Clym give up the Paris diamond business, rather than humble shopkeeping as he first planned, he gave himself more scope to emphasise the disparity between Clym's and the 'luxurious' Eustacia's world-views.) His sight deteriorates after his marriage to Eustacia and, like Endymion, he can cry: 'Before mine eyes thick films and shadows float' (II.323).

In the chapter which follows the eclipse episode, the jealous Mrs Yeobright's 'sharp words' foil Clym's attempt to bring her and Eustacia together. Instead, he goes to meet his lover alone on the heath:

> He was in a nest of vivid green. The ferny vegetation round him, though so abundant, was quite uniform: it was a grove of machine-made foliage, a world of green triangles with saw-edges, and not a single flower. The air was warm with a vaporous warmth, and the stillness was unbroken. Lizards, grass-hoppers, and ants were the only living things to be beheld. The scene seemed to belong to the ancient world of the carboniferous period, when the forms of plants were few, and of the fern kind; when there was neither bud nor blossom, nothing but a monotonous extent of leafage, amid which no bird sang. (III.5)

Isolated, and temporarily enclosed by these older and lower forms of plant and animal life, Clym is associated with the 'wretched wight' of Keats's 'La Belle Dame Sans Merci', in the unmarked quotation at the end of the paragraph:

> Oh, what can ail thee, knight-at-arms,
>   Alone and palely loitering?
> The sedge has withered from the lake,
>   And no birds sing! (1–4)

In this variation on the theme of the *femme fatale* and her victim, Hardy moves his protagonists from the Latmos of Rainbarrow to the 'elfin grot' (29) of the 'nest of vivid green' on the heath. As on the barrow, Eustacia regrets that 'the actual moment of a thing is so soon gone' and that her 'bliss . . . has been too intense and consuming'. Further echoes of Keats's poetry confirm this sense of the transitoriness of their love. They walk through the ferns together to 'the nether margin of the heath, where it became marshy, and merged in moorland'. The landscape is first reminiscent of 'Autumn':

The sun, resting on the horizon line, streamed across the ground from between copper-coloured and lilac clouds, stretched out in flats beneath a sky of pale soft green . . . . groups of wailing gnats shone out, rising upwards and dancing about like sparks of fire. (III.5)	While barrèd clouds bloom the soft-dying day, And touch the stubble-plains with rosy hue. Then in a wailful choir the small gnats mourn Among the river sallows, borne aloft Or sinking as the light wind lives or dies . . . .

(25–9)

When Eustacia leaves Clym, having agreed that they will be married in a fortnight's time, she moves through the landscape of 'La Belle Dame':

Clym watched her as she retired towards the sun. The luminous rays wrapped her up with her increasing distance, and the rustle of her dress over the sprouting sedge and grass died away. As he watched, the dead flat of the scenery overpowered him, though he was fully alive to the beauty of that untarnished early summer green which was worn for the nonce by the poorest blade. (III.5)

Symbolic of Clym's and Eustacia's love, the greenness of the foliage is temporary, 'worn for the nonce'. The 'sedge' will 'wither' by late autumn, when the 'squirrel's granary is full, / And the harvest's done' (7–8). Clym can now concentrate on his most immediate problems: 'Eustacia was now no longer the goddess but the woman to him, a being to fight for, support, help, be maligned for.' She is still, however, as elusively ethereal as La Belle Dame. Torn between the enchantment of the beautiful goddess-Eustacia and the practical problems posed by the woman-Eustacia, his comparative security already seems undermined. The last bald statement of the chapter in which the lovers decide to marry makes the point less powerfully than the parallels with Keats's studies of anguished love for immortal beauties: 'Whether Eustacia was to add one other to the list of those who love too hotly to love long and well, the forthcoming event was certainly a ready way of proving' (III.5).

Hardy is often at his best when he places his people in an environment to which they respond imaginatively. In the two chapters discussed above, that environment is associated with Keatsian landscapes in which human responses to elusive beauties are pathetically vulnerable. In both chapters, theme and scene become indistinguishable. Hardy's response to Keats, shared by the reader who recognises the parallels or what appear to be unmarked quotations, seem less a reading than a rewriting.

By the end of the subsequent (fourth) book, Clym has several reasons for keeping his eyes to the ground, rather than scrutinising the moon and Eustacia's face. His vision has deteriorated, ostensibly through excessive reading, forcing him to work at furze-cutting: 'His daily life was of a curious microscopic sort, his whole world being limited to a circuit of a few feet from his person' (IV.2). Eustacia's resentment causes a rift to develop between the couple which widens after the death of Clym's mother. Book Fifth, which is to end with the drownings in the weir, opens with a chapter motto: 'WHEREFORE IS LIGHT GIVEN TO HIM THAT IS IN MISERY.' Job 'cursed his day':

> Let the day perish wherein I was born . . . .
> Let that day be darkness . . . .
>
> Wherefore is light given to him that is in
> misery, and life unto the bitter in soul;
> Which long for death, but it cometh
> not . . . ?
>
> (Job 3.3–4, 20–21)

The narrative opens with Clym and Eustacia responding to the moon in quite different ways. One moonlit evening, about three

weeks after Mrs Yeobright's funeral, Eustacia 'reclined over the
garden gate as if to refresh herself awhile. The pale lunar touches
which make beauties of hags lent divinity to this face, already
beautiful' (V.1). Back in the house the 'pale, haggard' Clym lies
in the front bedroom where a shaded light is burning. (He now
more closely resembles the 'knight-at-arms' of 'La Belle Dame':
'Alone and palely loitering . . . / So haggard and so woe-begone'
(2,6).) When Eustacia tells him that 'the moon is shining beautifully' his reply is Job-like: 'Shining, is it? What's the moon to a
man like me? Let it shine – let anything be, so that I never see
another day.' Now that Cynthia's spell is broken, the estrangement of the couple is inevitable.

When the catastrophe comes, Eustacia herself cannot see the
moon. Setting out in the rain to meet Wildeve she is no longer the
sure-footed lover who used to hurry to trysts on the heath:
'Skirting the pool she followed the path towards Rainbarrow,
occasionally stumbling over twisted furze-roots, tufts of rushes,
or oozing lumps of fleshy fungi, which at this season lay
scattered about the heath like the rotten liver and lungs of some
colossal animal. The moon and stars were closed up by cloud and
rain to the degree of extinction' (V.7). The landscape seems as
grotesque as the waste land through which Browning's Roland
rides on his way to the Dark Tower. The manuscript (f.376) and
Belgravia version of the second sentence quoted, amended for the
first edition, lays more emphasis on the state of the heavens, but
with an exactness which Hardy may have thought too ponder-
ous: 'The moon and stars were closed up by cloud and rain, the
density amounting to a lunar and sidereal extinction' (*Belgravia*,
vol. 37, p. 14). Endymion's sense of foreboding, both in the
underworld and after he has met the Indian Maid, has a special
resonance when Wildeve and Eustacia drown in Shadwater
Weir. His 'journey homeward to habitual self' is like a 'mad
pursuing of the fog-born elf', whose 'flitting lantern . . . / Cheats
us into a swamp' (II.277–9). He sits with the Maid 'waiting for
some destruction' (IV.330) and later says to her: 'We might
embrace and die – voluptuous thought' (IV.759). Whereas Endymion's fears prove unfounded when the Indian Maid is
apotheosised as Cynthia and carries him off, 'spiritualized', to
'range / These forests' (IV.993–4), Eustacia dies in the pool and
Clym survives only as a 'thin, pallid' Lazarus (V.9). Eustacia
breaks the bonds of mortality only in death: 'They stood silently

looking upon Eustacia, who, as she lay there still in death, eclipsed all her living phases. Pallor did not include all the quality of her complexion, which seemed more than whiteness; it was *almost* light' (V.9; my emphasis). This Indian Maid never becomes a Cynthia.

Although Hardy's 'original conception of the story did not design a marriage between Thomasin and Venn' (Note to VI.3), his changes being dictated by 'certain circumstances of serial publication', he handled Venn's courtship in such a way as to heighten the pathos of Clym's early love for his goddess-Eustacia and her own frustration as a mere mortal living on Edgon Heath. After the Maypole dancing on the green in front of Bloom's-End, Venn tells Thomasin that he is waiting till the moon rises (VI.1). The subsequent scene parodies Clym's courtship of Eustacia at the time of the eclipse. As Venn looks for her glove, Thomasin watches him with eyes at once more acute and less visionary than her cousin's:

> Venn was still there. She watched the growth of the faint radiance appearing in the sky by the eastern hill, till presently the edge of the moon burst upwards and flooded the valley with light. Diggory's form was now distinct on the green; he was moving about in a bowed attitude, evidently scanning the grass for the precious missing article, walking in zigzags right and left till he should have passed over every foot of the ground.
>
> 'How very ridiculous!' Thomasin murmured to herself, in a tone which was intended to be satirical. 'To think that a man should be so silly as to go mooning about like that for a girl's glove! A respectable dairyman, too, and a man of money as he is now. What a pity!'

Unwittingly, Venn mimics Clym's stooping movements with his furze-hook. His 'mooning' is a pale imitation of Clym's lunar enchantment. That Thomasin's attitude is a healthy sign for a no-nonsense marriage only adds to one's sense of loss. Through the scene Hardy develops what formerly he had only stated in passing, when Thomasin set out on the night of the drownings: 'To her there were not, as to Eustacia, demons in the air, and malice in every bush and bough. The drops which lashed her face were not scorpions, but prosy rain; Egdon in the mass was no monster whatever, but impersonal open ground' (V.8). Eustacia's sublime conception of a grand passion leads to the weir, whereas Thomasin's common-sensical outlook leads to an Egdon wedding.

The triumph of normality over the sublime and the ideal conforms to the pattern of undermining which can be traced in the development of the novel's main themes. The *Return* can be read as an 'Antichristian Document', or as an early study of the 'Ache of Modernism', in which traditional values and beliefs are exposed as naive optimism in a hostile, godless universe.[6] Burkean sublimity gives way to prosiness,[7] and classical concepts of the heroic are shown to be 'displaced' in the modern age. Indeed, all Hardy's classical allusions should be read in the light of the paragraph which he inserts in his commentary on Clym at the beginning of the third book:

> The truth seems to be that a long line of disillusive centuries has permanently displaced the Hellenic idea of life, or whatever it may be called. What the Greeks only suspected we know well; what their Aeschylus imagined our nursery children feel. That old-fashioned revelling in the general situation grows less and less possible as we uncover the defects of natural laws, and see the quandary that man is in by their operation. (III.1)

Printed in the first edition, this is a shortened version of the paragraph in the manuscript (f.194) which appeared in the *Belgravia*:

> It has been said that the capacity to enjoy is at bottom identical with the capacity to produce; and the civilised world's lack of power to prolong in new combinations of art the old special beauties of men and gods, would imply that its sympathies lie secretly in other directions, despite any transient fashion. We have lost the true Hellenic eye, for this requires behind it the Hellenic idea of life; and a long line of disillusive centuries has permanently displaced that. The solecisms of ancient thought are the grammar of modern. What the Greeks only suspected we know well. . . . (*Belgravia*, vol. 35, p. 480)

(The *Belgravia* version also has 'cosmic' for 'natural' laws.) This earlier version specifically draws attention to the role of the modern artist, whereas the area of reference in the first and later editions is more general. In a novel in which the hero is dazzled and almost blinded, the phrase 'Hellenic eye' suggests limitations in both its creator and his creatures. (Hardy may have deleted the passage because it seemed pretentious and over explicit.) In the *Return*, the 'physical beauty' to which he refers in the previous paragraph is transient, perceived by eyes which become dim. The *Endymion* parallels in the novel mark a shift from visionary Romanticism (itself fragile in those hurried last lines in which Endymion is 'spiritualized') to a bleak vision of the 'defects of natural [or 'cosmic'] laws'. Those who stand upright on Egdon will be knocked down. Aspirations beyond the most subservient stance in relation to the heath will be ruthlessly crushed. A 'long line of disillusive centuries' belies the possibility of escape through apotheosis.

Hardy's handling of all the Keatsian parallels discussed above cannot be neatly classified as either the reworking of private literary sources or the establishment of a relationship between his novel and (public) adopted texts through allusion. *Endymion* is one of those intermediate works to which I referred in Chapter 2, being neither arcane nor familiar. Without the motto, even those Victorian readers of the *Return* who knew the poem would probably not have noticed parallels. Only the motto can be categorised as an unmistakable allusion, but its lack of ascription and its special independent nature (as a passage which is better known than the poem in which it is embedded) make its putative function as an indicator of a parallel text questionable. What I have called the unmarked quotations from 'La Belle Dame' and 'Autumn' ('no bird sang', 'sedge' and 'wailing gnats') are extremely flimsy and could easily be missed. Indeed, it could be argued that they are not unmarked quotations at all, but merely echoes, fragments of sources which Hardy was consciously or unconsciously reworking or developing as he wrote. If the motto had been ascribed, the parallel *Endymion* passages more clearly indicated through allusion, and the echoes of 'La Belle Dame' and 'Autumn' made marked quotations, one could confidently assert that Hardy as narrator used quotations from Keats in order to focus the reader's attention on the demythologising of Romantic literary tradition, idealising and visionary, which is one of the novel's major concerns. As it is, his highly illuminating use of Keatsian themes must have been missed by many of the novel's admirers.

III

Disguise is often associated with changes in character and role in the *Return*. For example, Clym's relationship with Eustacia moves into a new and difficult phase when the 'man from Paris' is 'disguised by his leather accoutrements' as a furze-cutter (IV.2); and Thomasin seems to say more than she knows when she first sees the reddleman restored to his former whiteness: 'I thought you were the ghost of yourself' (VI.1). Early in *Tess* the important theme of change, and particularly change of form or substance (metamorphosis), is introduced through references to Ovid's *Metamorphoses*.

On the night of her seduction, Tess is a spectator at a dance in Chaseborough. She sets out from Trantridge 'just before sunset, when yellow lights struggle with blue shades in hair-like lines' (10). (Crucial events in the novel often occur around the time when day and night 'struggle' for supremacy, in the uncertain hours when light changes to dark, and vice versa. Tess, Angel and Alec all tend to become more sensitive and responsive to change at dawn or dusk.) Having completed her marketing, Tess finds her way to a hay-trusser's outhouse, where a 'private little jig' is being held, and at first thinks 'a mist of yellow radiance' to be 'illuminated smoke': 'But on drawing nearer she perceived that it was a cloud of dust, lit by candles within the outhouse, whose beams upon the haze carried forward the outline of the doorway into the wide night of the garden.' She sees 'indistinct forms' dancing in the dust:

> Through this floating, fusty *débris* of peat and hay, mixed with the perspirations and warmth of the dancers, and form-ing together a sort of vegeto-human pollen, the muted fiddles feebly pushed their notes, in marked contrast to the spirit with which the measure was trodden out. They coughed as they danced, and laughed as they coughed. Of the rushing couples there could barely be discerned more than the high lights – the indistinctness shaping them to satyrs clasping nymphs – a

multiplicity of Pans whirling a multiplicity of Syrinxes; Lotis attempting to elude Priapus, and always failing.

That the references in the last sentence are specifically to Ovid's *Metamorphoses* is confirmed in the subsequent paragraph: 'Could Trantridge in two or three short hours have metamorphosed itself thus madly!'[8] There is also a reference to 'some Sileni of the throng' who 'sat on benches and hay-trusses by the wall'.

Tess's uneasiness at the dance is understandable. She seems to have stumbled upon a kind of Bacchic ritual, during which the villagers she knows so well appear to be transformed into satyrs and nymphs under the influence of 'liquor' and spirited dancing. In the *Metamorphoses*, Mercury tells how a nymph called Syrinx kept her virginity by eluding satyrs, and avoided capture by Pan by changing herself into a 'handful of marsh reeds', which he then used as his pipes (I). Later, Iole tells the stories of some of those who failed to escape the numerous rapacious figures who haunt the poem. Her half-sister, Dryope, was 'assaulted by the god who rules Delphi and Delos' and later turned into a tree (IX). The immediate cause of this typically sudden and terrifying metamorphosis was her innocent plucking of blossoms from a tree which dripped blood, because 'the nymph Lotis, fleeing from the obscenities of Priapus, had been turned into the lotus tree, changing her appearance, but keeping her own name' (IX). Tess is to be seduced by Alec and later to go through a series of metamorphoses. Whereas she seems an alien at the dance and intuitively holds back when invited to join in, the male onlookers enjoy the spectacle: the 'Sileni' emulate Bacchus's corpulent and drunken old tutor (*Metamorphoses*, XI), and Alec, unnoticed before, laughs loudly when the couples fall in a heap. Following the Ovidian allusions quoted above, his stealthy arrival on the scene, where he stands behind Tess, alone, poses an obvious threat to her.

The theme of change, which these references to Ovid introduce, proves to be central to Hardy's portrayal of Tess's relationships with both Alec and Angel: new stages of her life are marked by rapid changes, and meanwhile Alec and Angel are changing, making her decisions increasingly difficult. Following her seduction and the birth and death of Sorrow, Tess speculates on her own death day: 'Almost at a leap Tess thus changed from simple girl to complex woman. Symbols of reflectiveness passed into her face, and a note of tragedy at times into her voice. Her eyes grew larger and more eloquent' (15). Her 'Rally' (Phase the Third) is dependent upon a change of scene and other allied changes. As she enters the Valley of the Great Dairies on her way to Talbothays, 'either the change in the quality of the air from heavy to light, or the sense of being amid new scenes where there were no invidious eyes upon her, sent up her spirits wonderfully. . . . Her face had latterly changed with changing states of mind, continually fluctuating between beauty and ordinariness, according as the thoughts were gay or grave' (16). She 'fluctuates' between the reality of the past (Alec and the death of Sorrow) and the ideality of the future (Angel and the 'luminous' dawn meetings at the dairy). In high spirits and at her most beautiful she is ready for Angel, who first takes notice of the new dairymaid when he overhears her talking about the soul: 'I do know that our souls can be made to go outside our bodies when we are alive. . . . A very easy way to feel 'em go . . . is to lie on the grass at night and look straight up at some big bright star; and, by fixing your mind upon it, you will soon find that you are hundreds and hundreds o' miles away from your body, which you don't seem to want at all' (18).

Tess's interest in the soul going 'outside our bodies' is rooted in her awareness of 'states of consciousness' within herself which are higher than the responses of the workaday senses, and in her need to escape from past miseries associated with her own body. In the famous evening scene in which she is attracted to Angel by the sound of his harp, she is frightened by the 'inquisitive eyes' of trees which seem to have human life (as in the *Metamorphoses*) and says to Angel: 'But *you*, sir, can raise up dreams with your music, and drive all such horrid fancies away!' (19). (The manuscript reads: '"But you, sir – *you*," she exclaimed with almost bitter envy; "you can raise up dreams"' (f. 137).) What seems magical to Tess, however, is in fact rather poorly executed music on an old second-hand harp. Although she is apparently apotheosised in the light of dawn at Talbothays, looking 'ghostly', 'a visionary essence of woman', and 'no longer the milkmaid', her features soon become 'simply feminine' as it grows lighter: they 'changed from those of a divinity who could confer bliss to those of a being who craved it' (20). Moments of communion with Angel, when surrounded by natural beauty, are as fleeting as the basis of their relationship is insecure.

The tension between Angel's appreciation of Tess's 'incarnate' beauty (27) and his 'more spiritual than animal' nature (31) is echoed in Tess's love for him, which has 'hardly a touch of earth' in it (31) and yet relies upon his physical presence for security. Her feelings at her wedding reflect both her sense of wonder and her sense of insecurity: 'she unconsciously inclined herself towards him . . . to assure herself that he was really there' (33), while at the same time feeling that she was 'a sort of celestial person, who owed her being to poetry'. Tess expects to experience some great change in her newly married state: a different kind of response to life at Angel's side. In front of the fire, before the fatal confession, Angel's family gems seem to be catalysts in the metamorphosis of the light: 'Tess's face and neck reflected the same warmth, which each gem turned into an Aldebaran or a Sirius – a constellation of white, red, and green flashes, that interchanged their hues with her every pulsation' (34). Ominously, each gem gives a 'sinister wink like a toad's' immediately before she confesses. After her narrative, the major change which has taken place is quite different from that which she expected in her new marital state:

> . . . the complexion even of external things seemed to suffer transmutation as her announcement progressed. The fire in the grate looked impish – demoniacally funny, as if it did not care in the least about her strait. The fender grinned idly, as if it too did not care. The light from the water-bottle was merely engaged in a chromatic problem. All material objects around announced their irresponsibility with terrible iteration. And yet nothing had changed since the moments when he had been kissing her; or rather, nothing in the substance of things. But the essence of things had changed. (35)

The implied vulnerability of Tess in the Talbothays chapters, when she fluctuates between different states as beautiful dairymaid and visionary deity, now becomes a cruel reality. In front of the fire everything that surrounds her is 'irresponsible' in its lack of 'care' for her strait. The change in the 'complexion' of inanimate objects is disturbingly ambiguous in its essentiality rather than substantiality. The informed Victorian reader would probably have associated the word 'transmutation' with the work of Darwin and possibly that of other nineteenth-century theorists, including Lamarck, Huxley and Spencer, rather than with the old alchemical connotations of the word.[9] Hardy was forcibly struck by the fact that Darwinian selection operates in a world which coldly looks on, allowing natural forces to have full sway.[10] After her confession, Tess's decline from wife to poverty-stricken field-worker, to adulteress, and eventually to murderess, takes place in a hostile world in which what will be will be, according to local lore and the laws of biological science.

Angel's response to Tess's plea for forgiveness suggests that for him 'the essence of things' had indeed changed: 'O Tess, forgiveness does not apply to the case! You were one person; now you are another' (35). He adds that the woman he has been loving is not her but 'another woman' in her 'shape'. Angel thinks in terms of essential change rather than metamorphosis (change of substance), whereas Tess conceives of a 'me, my very self' which can stay the same through 'all changes, all disgraces'. Angel's attitude reflects the nature of his love for her, described in an earlier chapter: 'a love more especially inclined to the imaginative and ethereal; it was a fastidious emotion which could jealously guard the loved one against his very self' (31). After the estrangement, Hardy develops these comments, saying that his love is 'ethereal to a fault, imaginative to impracticability', and that with 'these natures, corporeal presence is something less appealing than corporeal absence; the latter creating an ideal presence that conveniently drops the defects of the real' (36). Like Angel, Tess has nurtured a love in which there is 'hardly a touch of earth' (31). But in Angel's case such a love cannot stand the shock of a sudden revelation of the grossest 'defects of the real'.

After this change in their relationship, Tess tries to achieve some kind of equilibrium in a world in which the men in her life fluctuate in their attitudes towards her. She tries to navigate among wandering rocks. At a purely practical level she can accommodate change with the resignation of one who was poor before she married, taking work as it is offered to her and gradually sinking down the scale of agricultural employment. In order to protect herself from admiring men she disguises her beauty by cutting off her eyebrows and wearing a headscarf, to become 'a fieldwoman pure and simple' (42). She can survive by taking a stoical view of her lot as she hacks swedes at Flintcomb-

Ash. It is only when Alec crosses her path again that she faces a real threat. Phase the Sixth ('The Convert') opens with a description of Alec's religious conversion: 'It was less a reform than a transfiguration. The former curves of sensuousness were now modulated to lines of devotional passion. The lip-shapes that had meant seductiveness were now made to express supplication; the glow on the cheek that yesterday could be translated as riotousness was evangelized to-day into the splendour of pious rhetoric' (45). Alec soon reverts to type, however, blaming Tess for rekindling his passion for her. When he appears at the rick on which Tess is working he is 'changed' in 'attire and aspect': 'It was obvious at a glance that the original *Weltlust* had come back; that he had restored himself, as nearly as a man could do who had grown three or four years older, to the old jaunty, slap-dash guise under which Tess had first known her admirer, and cousin so-called' (47). This Protean figure lurches from a Pauline to a satanic identity, first wearing 'old-fashioned whiskers' and 'half-clerical' dress as an Evangelical preacher (45) and later reassuming the stage-villain costume in which he haunts Tess. When he adopts yet another disguise, a 'long smockfrock', in order to surprise her on her father's allotment, he explicitly compares himself to Satan tempting Eve and quotes *Paradise Lost*, which he used to know quite well when he was 'theological' (50). Tess is not only forced to adopt disguises in order to protect herself, but also has to 'read' or 'translate' Alec's, which sometimes signal a profound though transient change, but are often only skin-deep.

In the final Phase of the novel ('Fulfilment') every change in the characters' lives seems double-edged. When Angel returns to Emminster Vicarage from Brazil, his mother cries: 'O, it is not Angel – not my son – the Angel who went away', and his father is 'shocked to see him', so 'reduced' is that figure from its former contours by worry and the bad season that Clare has experienced (53). It is only a reduced Clare, however, made lower than the Angels, who can respond to Tess's pleas to return to her. At their meeting on the threshold of The Herons in Sandbourne he is acutely aware that he has 'altered', and finds Tess not at all as he expects to see her, 'bewilderingly otherwise, indeed' (55). He is reduced, while she is disguised as Alec's mistress, 'loosely wrapped in a cashmere dressing-gown of gray-white, embroidered in half-mourning tints', and wearing 'slippers of the same hue'. At the end of the chapter, in a crucial sentence which he added in the Wessex Novels edition of 1895, Hardy makes explicit the formerly implicit impression that Tess experiences death-in-life with Alec: Angel 'had a vague consciousness of one thing, though it was not clear to him till later; that his original Tess had spiritually ceased to recognize the body before him as hers – allowing it to drift, like a corpse upon the current, in a direction dissociated from its living will' (55). This added sentence echoes Tess's thoughts on the soul going 'outside our bodies' at Talbothays (18) and her abandonment to her fate as Angel carried her over the swollen river Froom at Wellbridge (37). The change which Angel observes in his 'original Tess' is both reductive and beneficial, as it gives him the opportunity of rationalising his new response to her. Once she has murdered Alec, Tess herself is as good as dead, and when she and Angel move inland they are bound to be captured. At Stonehenge she reaches both her zenith and her nadir. A tragic heroine sacrificed on an altar 'older than the centuries', she is also a pathetically small figure as she sleeps, surrounded by men who have come to arrest her: 'her breathing now was quick and small, like that of a lesser creature than a woman' (58). A trapped animal, she awaits violent death, the final great change.

It is clear, then, that the theme of change is of fundamental importance in *Tess*, and that the Ovidian references in the Chaseborough dance chapter fulfil an important function as thematic pointers. (I was first alerted to the theme by the allusions.) Yet the Chaseborough dance section of *Tess* was omitted from the serial version in the *Graphic* and published separately as part of Hardy's sketch, 'Saturday Night in Arcady' (Pan's domain), in a more liberal weekly, the *National Observer* (14 November 1891). Then, unlike most of the other bowdlerisations for the *Graphic* version, the dance episode was not restored to the text in the first book edition, and was inserted only in the Wessex edition of 1912, when Hardy claimed in a preface that the relevant pages of the manuscript had been previously 'overlooked'. A close student of the manuscript and all published versions of *Tess*, J. T. Laird, writes: 'Just why Hardy omitted this richly Ovidian section is not adequately explained by his note in the 1912 edition. . . . Indeed . . . they were *not* "overlooked", although it is not easy to understand Hardy's motive in attempting to conceal the fact.'[11] It is equally difficult to see why he eventually decided to restore the section in the 1912 edition, in spite of the fact that he explained his reasoning when he told his publisher that '⅓ of a chapter' in the manuscript had been 'accidentally omitted from all the volume forms of the story': 'I don't know if it would be a good commercial stroke to keep this private till we bring out a new edition of the book, and then announce it in literary paragraphs, etc. Nobody, of course, would remember reading it in the National Observer' (Laird, p. 19). As a 'good commercial stroke' would have been just as effective in an earlier edition, why did Hardy conceal the 'accidentally omitted' section for so long, assuming that the omission was not accidental, as Laird has shown?

One small but significant change in the manuscript may provide a clue. Angel Clare's famous response to the story of the fiddler and the bull ('It's a curious story; it carries us back to mediaeval times, when faith was a living thing!' (17)) was inserted in the manuscript above these deleted words: "Quite an Orpheus!" — story!" (f. 119). Hardy may have wanted to make the Orphean parallels associated with Angel implicit rather than explicit, and therefore removed the allusion, inserting in its place the statement which underlines the loss of faith which character- ised his own age. He may have had a similar motive for omitting the passage which includes the all-important Ovidian allusions. Ovidian metamorphosis is only one of several kinds of change which are explored in *Tess*, and the *Metamorphoses* is not a 'parallel text' to be 'read' alongside the novel, in the sense that *Endymion* can be 'read' as a parallel text in the *Return*. The numerous words which Hardy uses to decribe *change*, itself a common word in *Tess*, indicate the areas of reference which he covers or touches on in the novel. Protean *change*, Ovidian *metamorphosis*, spiritual *apotheosis* and *transfiguration*, Evangelical *conversion*, and biological *transmutation* all figure in the novel. This variety of terms provides a further clue to Hardy's reasons for omitting the dance episode: he may have wanted to avoid encouraging the reader to focus exclusively on one kind of change.

What was lost when the episode was omitted in early editions, apart from the intrinsic merits of the episode itself? Alec's brief conversion from his Arcadian lustfulness to the ethics of the New Testament was less precisely charted; the effects of the dance and the Ovidian allusions as plot pointers to Tess's subsequent rape in the Chase were lost; and, perhaps most significantly, the thematic key-note of the novel was less clearly struck. Hardy's initial reasons for omitting the episode and his later motives for not replacing it were probably mixed, being based on anxiety and literary judgment. The episode may have seemed too 'strong' for most novel readers of 1891. Furthermore, the fact that it was written around the Ovidian allus:--- ; would have made its omission typical of Hardy's editing of his own novel. But above all, I suspect that he may have wanted his readers to respond to his text, the end product of a response to numerous pressures, including his knowledge of the *Metamorphoses*, without one particular source being made an adopted text through allusion. In other words, what he made of the source may have been more important to him than the way in which the allusions operated in the text. If this *was* a major consideration which affected the decision to omit the passage, we can see in retrospect that Hardy was right to change his mind in 1912, as the novel is the richer for its inclusion.

Both the *Return* and *Tess* explore the tensions between the real and the ideal, and the relations between change, identity, and disguise. The focus on Keatsian themes and images is never quite clear in the *Return*, probably as a result of Hardy's uneasiness in his handling of 'private' sources and in his use of the convention of allusion to 'public' adopted texts. In *Tess*, Hardy seems to have been unsure whether to alert his readers to the literary parallels he exploits in the novel. The reinstated Ovidian passage in the Wessex edition of the later novel does, however, prepare the reader to attend to the theme of metamorphosis and to be more fully alive to the vulnerability and instability of the chief protagonists in a world in which the 'defects of natural laws' operate upon the 'defects of the real'.

10
Conclusion

I

Before commenting generally on the art of allusion in Victorian fiction, I want to mention certain broad developments in early twentieth-century fiction. The most important development is related to the self-conscious playfulness of much of this fiction, including some of the short stories and novellas, published in literary magazines at the turn of the century, which mark a transition from late Victorian to early modernist themes and techniques, including the use of allusion. Among these, James's most famous novella, *The Turn of the Screw* (1898), is a good starting point for any study of twentieth-century fiction, being problematic in its exploration of ambiguities which are different in kind from those of Conrad's more obviously seminal *Heart of Darkness* (1902). James himself spoke disparagingly of his story, describing it as 'essentially a pot-boiler' and, more interestingly, a *'jeu d'esprit'*.[1] Recognising the complexity of the work, however, many critics have trusted the tale and not the teller, and have explored the ambiguities which suggest themselves once the governess's sanity, and thus the validity of her interpretation of events, are questioned. The names of the two schools of criticism which have emerged, the 'apparitionist' and the 'non-apparitionist', reflect the central ambiguity of the story. As an agnostic non-apparitionist, I think James is playing with his reader's expectations in the story, and that one aspect of this play is his handling of Gothic conventions, such as the use of Bly, a remote country house, as the setting for the governess's story. Most important from my point of view are the parallels with and possible references to *Jane Eyre*. I say possible references be-

159

cause they are as difficult to pin down as the governess's narrative itself, which, as Douglas says in the introductory section of the story, *'won't* tell, not in any literal, vulgar way'.[2] Thus a straightforward reader-narrator contract is replaced by an invitation to a game of chess between reader and narrator in *The Turn of the Screw*, as it is in Kipling's 'Wireless' (1902) and 'Proofs of Holy Writ' (1934), short stories in which the writer plays with allusion as a means by which to reconstruct acts of creative writing.

Broadly speaking, this twentieth-century predilection for games or puzzles,[3] shared by writers as various as Joyce, Beckett and Borges, is closer in spirit to the eighteenth century than to the Victorian period. In *Tom Jones*, for example, Fielding's gnomic quotations from the Classics and his mock-heroic classical parallels not only generate a sense of what Johnson called 'community of mind' between writer and reader but also implicitly test the reader's knowledge. Pound's observation that 'Ulysses is, presumably, as unrepeatable as Tristram Shandy' encourages comparison of the novels, and a list of similarities between them would include a playfulness of allusion.[4] Whereas allusion tends to have a focusing effect in Victorian fiction, encouraging the reader to concentrate on the central themes of novels, in *Tristram Shandy* and *Ulysses*, the high points of formal self-consciousness in their respective periods, we are treated to virtuoso performances in the art of allusion, as daring and baffling as other aspects of their narratives. As in that other syncretic work of 1922, Eliot's *The Waste Land*, a kind of cultural collage is created by Joyce in *Ulysses* through the juxtaposition of quotations from and references to a wide variety of adopted texts. Unlike his Victorian precursors, Joyce brings a vast array of disparate elements together under the one big top of a novel in which, in Pound's words, we find 'sheer whoops and hoop-las and trapeze turns of technique'.

It would be wrong, however, to assert that all allusion in major early twentieth-century fiction is playful. Lawrence, of course, like Carlyle and Dickens before him, based the prose style of his most deeply felt prophetic passages on the Bible and drew upon biblical texts in developing his symbolism. For example, God's covenant with Noah in Genesis 9 echoes through *The Rainbow* (1915), the novel in which Lawrence discovered new ways of exploiting old fictional conventions. Less obviously, Virginia

Woolf's art of allusion also grew out of nineteenth-century conventions.[5] What is new and exciting in Woolf is the way in which she experiments with techniques which were not new in themselves. For example, the famous line from the song in *Cymbeline*, 'Fear no more the heat o' the sun', is musical in its repetitiveness in *Mrs Dalloway* (1925), ringing through the novel like the chimes of Big Ben, but suggesting dimensions of time which no clock can register. An analysis of the functions of allusion in modern fiction might make a good starting point for a study of what has been called the 'new mix' of Joyce's and Woolf's treatments of the 'flow of human experience' through a reworking of realistic conventions,[6] but my own concern is with allusion in Victorian fiction, on which I now want to make some concluding comments.

II

In my earlier chapters I have often found it necessary to remind the reader of the sequence of events in those parts of my selected novels which I consider to be particularly important. I hope I have thus been able to preserve some sense of the necessarily sequential way in which we respond to allusions as we read these fictional narratives. I have suggested that even widely separated quotations from and references to the same adopted text can have an accumulative effect, later allusions 'reactivating' earlier allusions. Perhaps the most characteristic accumulative effect of allusion in Victorian novels is the establishment of a symbolic pattern or structure within an adopted text through the development of some kind of relationship with an adopted (often parallel) text. Sets of allusions to a single adopted text can provide the analogical matrix which shapes part of a novel, either overtly (the *Pilgrim's Progress* in *Jane Eyre*) or semi-covertly (*Endymion* in *The Return of the Native*). On the other hand, allusions to a wide range of adopted texts can contribute to an adoptive text's central symbolism, as in *Middlemarch*. It is worth remembering Harold Bloom's point that for Bacon 'allusion' meant 'any symbolic likening, whether in allegory, parable or metaphor' (see p. 3), for the boundaries between the functions of allusion and symbolism are often difficult to define. When related sets of allusions establish symbolic relations between adopted texts and adoptive works of realistic fiction, shapings other than the linear sequence of the reading experience assume major importance. I will illustrate what I mean by citing the views of a modern critic who is not happy with the way in which certain recent criticism of Victorian fiction has developed.

Peter Garrett has argued that modern readings of Victorian 'multiple narratives' have tended to 'reduce multiplicity to unity by thematic abstraction and analogy'.[7] He cites a number of examples, including Daleski's *Dickens and the Art of Analogy* (1970), adding:

> The use of visual or spatial metaphors is a common feature in such interpretations, revealing the tendency of thematic criticism to spatialize narrative, to rearrange its elements according to patterns of similarity and contrast. Every narrative permits or invites this kind of reading to some extent, usually to a greater extent as narrative order departs from linear chronology, and the inevitable discontinuity of multiple narratives, with their repeated breaks and transitions, reduces the importance of sequence and increases that of typological or analogical relationships. The essential characteristic of such relationships, however, is that in themselves they have no necessary order: the patterns which exponents of thematic unity describe are created by the act of interpretation, by the critic's choice of terms and emphasis. (Garrett, pp. 2–3)

Now Garrett is surely right in insisting that Victorian novels with double (*Vanity Fair*) or multiple (*Middlemarch*) narrative lines have a 'dialogical' rather than 'monological' form; that they are 'organized by a double logic, a dialogue of structural perspectives' (Garrett, pp. 5–6). However, in his earlier comments on the tendency of thematic critics to rearrange the elements of narrative, he seems to understate the point that all readers, critical and non-critical, rearrange those elements as they read. Readers attend to the sequence or sequences of realistic plots and, at the same time, recognise other patterns suggested by recurring and possibly widely separated elements of narrative.

When allusion or symbolism triggers associations in our minds as we read (necessarily sequentially), both the text which we are reading and our store of accumulated associations are reshaped. T. S. Eliot discussed the importance of this kind of

reshaping for the creative writer in 'Tradition and the Individual
Talent' (1919). My present concern is with the reader of creative
writing. As a reader responds to sets of allusions within a
narrative, he exercises his memory in a manner similar to that
described by Sammy Mountjoy in Golding's *Free Fall* (1959):

> Time is not to be laid out endlessly like a row of bricks. That
> straight line from the first hiccup to the last gasp is a dead
> thing. Time is two modes. The one is an effortless perception
> native to us as water to the mackerel. The other is a memory, a
> sense of shuffle fold and coil, of that day mirroring this, or
> those three set apart, exceptional and out of the straight line
> altogether. (1)

We read the words, phrases and sentences of a text like a row of
bricks, and, as we proceed, the shuffle, fold and coil of memory
and association rearranges and unifies the text, whether it be
monological or dialogical.

Now the memories and associations which we bring to a text
are obviously determined partly by our previous reading and our
present expectations as readers. Jonathan Culler writes:

> A text can be a poem only because certain possibilities exist
> within the tradition; it is written in relation to other poems. A
> sentence of English can have meaning only by virtue of its
> relations to other sentences within the conventions of the
> language. The communicative intention presupposes listeners
> who know the language. And similarly, a poem presupposes
> conventions of reading which the author may work against,
> which he can transform, but which are the conditions of
> possibility of his discourse.[8]

The particular convention of allusion in nineteenth-century fiction which I have been discussing presupposes readers who
'know the language' of that convention, and it is hardly surpris-
ing to find that changes in the use of allusion in later Victorian
fiction parallel changes in the novelists' concept of their audience, and thus in the scope of what I have called the reader-
narrator contract. In *Jane Eyre*, *Mary Barton* and *Hard Times*,
novels all published in the 1840s and 1850s, allusions evoke
associations which would have been shared by their writers and

early Victorian readers. Most of the references to and quotations from the Bible, *Paradise Lost* and the *Pilgrim's Progress* in *Jane Eyre* were probably as readily recognisable as its Gothic conventions and the parody of religious hypocrisy in the Lowood chapters. The middle-class reader was brought face to face with working-class radicalism articulated through Burns and New Testament texts in *Mary Barton*, adopted texts which were almost certainly familiar to him. Directly appealed to in the last paragraph of *Hard Times*, the reader who recognised the apocalyptic allusions in the novel could see that the novel's themes were larger than its local social-problem concerns. George Eliot's handling of allusion in *Middlemarch*, published seventeen years after *Hard Times*, showed signs of an awareness of a specialised, highly educated readership, although her revisions, through which allusions were made clearer, may suggest that she still had a wider readership in mind as she quoted.[9] The heavy use of marked quotations in *Robert Elsmere* is one of the more outmoded features of a novel in which Mary Ward traces the development of her own century for scholars and 'the populace' alike. Meredith's allusions in *The Egoist* are of a different order, being playfully poetic or referentially oblique, and would not have made the novel any more accessible to what Margaret Oliphant called 'the multitude'; and Hardy's uncertainties concerning overt allusion and the covert reworking of inherited literary forms and themes may reflect uncertainties concerning his side of the reader-narrator contract.

Hardy's uncertain handling of allusion obviously contrasts with the confident use of the convention in *Jane Eyre*, *Mary Barton* and *Hard Times*. When allusion becomes a *theme* in *Middlemarch* and *The Egoist* it is as if the convention, like other techniques in Victorian fiction, is being scrutinised and reassessed in the novels, which often seem to be reworkings of earlier nineteenth-century themes. Similarly, Eliot's and Hardy's explorations of the relationship between the real and the ideal, a typically nineteenth-century dichotomy, make explicit what is implicit in all the novels I have discussed: that allusion helps to control the distance between modern realistic prose narrative, with its particular people, places and events, and established types and forms. Famous literary and biblical types and analogues are evoked directly, confidently and unselfconsciously in the early novels, helping the reader to understand the fiction by indicating the modes and conventions which novelists are adapting for their own purposes. Apart from *Robert Elsmere*, the later novels seem to have been written in the knowledge that the presuppositions on which Victorian realism was based should be reassessed, and that, in Hardy's words, the civilised world does indeed lack the power to 'prolong in new combinations of art the old special beauties of men and gods' (see p. 148). Evocative of those old special beauties, allusion is increasingly used ironically as the tension between the real and the ideal becomes explicit and problematic in a post-Darwinian world, where faith in God and belief in the value and purpose of human life is increasingly under threat. Unselfconsciousness in the handling of allusion tends to give way to self-consciousness, directness to obliqueness. Changes in the art of allusion in Victorian fiction mirror changes in both the genre and the age.

References

CHAPTER 1

[1] E. E. Kellett, *Literary Quotation and Allusion* (Cambridge, 1933), pp. 28, 11.

[2] Herman Meyer, *The Poetics of Quotation in the European Novel* (1961), translated by Theodore and Yetta Ziolkowski (Princeton, 1968), p. 3.

[3] Harold Bloom, *A Map of Misreading* (New York, 1975), p. 125. Compare *The Anxiety of Influence: A Theory of Poetry* (New York and London, 1973), *Kabbalah and Criticism* (New York, 1975), and *Poetry and Repression: Revisionism from Blake to Stevens* (New Haven and London, 1976).

[4] Ziva Ben-Porat, 'The Poetics of Literary Allusion', *PTL: A Journal for Descriptive Poetics and Theory in Literature*, 1 (1976), 105–28.

[5] 'Plato; or, the Philosopher', *Representative Men* (1850), in *The Complete Prose Works of Ralph Waldo Emerson*, edited by G. T. Bettany, Minerva Library (London, 1898), p. 170.

[6] For dictionary definitions of *allusion* which include the meaning of a direct reference see the *Universal Dictionary of the English Language*, edited by Henry Cecil Wyld (London, 1931), p. 27, and the *Supplement to the Oxford English Dictionary*, edited by R. W. Birchfield, 3 vols (Oxford, 1972–), I, 66.

[7] Techniques are being developed by A. Q. Morton, and colleagues in the Department of Computer Science at the University of Edinburgh, whereby authors can be identified by their use of recurring collocations. For a discussion of the use of computers and concordances, see D. R. Tallentire, 'Towards an archive of lexical norms. A proposal', in *The Computer and Literary Studies*, edited by A. J. Aitken, R. W. Bailey, and N. Hamilton-Smith (Edinburgh, 1973), pp. 39–60. See also S. Michaelson and A. Q. Morton, 'Positional stylometry', in *The Computer and Literary Studies*, pp. 69–83.

[8] See W. K. Wimsatt, Junior, *The Verbal Icon: Studies in the Meaning of Poetry* (1954; reprinted, London, 1970), pp. 11–12.

[9] W. K. Wimsatt, Junior, 'Genesis: A Fallacy Revisited', in *The Disciplines of Criticism: Essays in Literary Theory, Interpretation, and History*, edited by Peter Demetz, Thomas Greene, and Lowry Nelson, Junior (New Haven and London, 1968), pp. 193–225 (pp. 224–5).

[10] Wimsatt, *The Verbal Icon*, p. 10.

CHAPTER 2

[1] *Boswell's Life of Johnson*, Oxford Standard Authors (London, 1953), p. 1143.

[2] Review of *Jane Eyre* in *Fraser's Magazine*, 40 (1849), 691–4 (p. 692). See *The Brontës: The Critical Heritage*, edited by Miriam Allott (London and Boston, 1974), p. 152.

[3] Richard Stang, *The Theory of the Novel in England 1850–1870* (New York and London, 1959), p. 50.

[4] Charles Birchenough, *History of Elementary Education*, second edition (London, 1925), p. 372. See Richard D. Altick, *The English Common Reader* (Chicago and London, 1957), p. 161.

[5] Owen Chadwick, *The Victorian Church*, second edition, 2 vols, *An Ecclesiastical History of England*, VII and VIII, edited by J. C. Dickinson (London, 1970–2), II, 129.

[6] *The Letters and Private Papers of William Makepeace Thackeray*, edited by Gordon N. Ray, 4 vols (London and Cambridge, Mass., 1945–6), II, 282.

[7] George Watson, *The English Ideology: Studies in the Language of Victorian Politics* (London, 1973), p. 119.

[8] R. K. Webb, 'The Victorian Reading Public', in *From Dickens to Hardy*, edited by Boris Ford, revised edition, Pelican Guide to English Literature, VI (Harmondsworth, 1969), pp. 205–26 (p. 207).

[9] Kenneth L. Moler, *Jane Austen's Art of Allusion* (Lincoln, USA, 1968), pp. 1–2.

[10] See Earl R. Wasserman, *Shelley: A Critical Reading* (Baltimore, 1971), pp. 282–4.

[11] Tom B. Haber, 'The Chapter-Tags in the Waverley Novels', *PMLA*, 45 (1930), 1140–9 (p. 1146).

[12] *The Letters of Mrs Gaskell*, edited by J. A. V. Chapple and Arthur Pollard (Manchester, 1966), p. 542.

[13] Although most critics have agreed that Branderham's text is Matthew 18.22, the presence of Zillah the servant in chapter 3 could be said to suggest a secondary adopted text, Genesis 4.24, the biblical Zillah being one of Lamech's two wives (Genesis 4.19). Logical and associative connections are dislocated as the reader, like Lockwood, hopes to keep the inhabitants of the Heights at bay, but finds that the inner life of reading and analysis, and of dreaming, is more confusing and disturbing than is the 'real' life of the house. For the critical debate over the Branderham text see the following articles in *Nineteenth-Century Fiction*: Ruth M. Adams, '*Wuthering Heights*: The Land East of Eden', 13 (1958–9), 58–62; Edgar F. Shannon, Junior, 'Lockwood's Dreams and the Exegesis of *Wuthering Heights*', 14 (1959–60), 95–109; Vereen M. Bell, '*Wuthering Heights* and the Unforgivable Sin', 17 (1962–3), 188–91; Ronald E. Fine, 'Lockwood's Dreams and the Key to *Wuthering Heights*', 24 (1969–70), 16–30; William A. Madden, '*Wuthering Heights*: The Binding of Passion', 27 (1972–3), 127–54. See also J. Hillis Miller, *The Disappearance of God: Five Nineteenth-Century Writers* (Cambridge, Mass. and London, 1963), pp. 187–91.

CHAPTER 3

[1] For a different treatment of this aspect of the novel see Jane Millgate's important article on 'Jane Eyre's Progress', *English Studies Supplement*, 1969,

xxi–xxix. Although parts of Millgate's discussion overlap with mine, she does not comment on the crucial passages describing Jane's approach to Moor House or on the nature of Jane's interpretation of Rochester's cry.

[2] Jane Millgate shows that Jane respects Rivers, but feels in no sense inferior to him: 'She had, after all, rejected, as the ultimate temptation, the sanctuary of the Celestial City at a time when she had not yet finally located her own.' Millgate, pp. xxviii–xxix.

[3] 'Charlotte determined to make her heroine plain, small, and unattractive, in defiance of the accepted canon.' Elizabeth Gaskell, *The Life of Charlotte Brontë*, edited by Alan Shelston, Penguin English Library (Harmondsworth, 1975), p. 308.

[4] Tom Winnifrith, *The Brontës*, Masters of World Literature Series, edited by Louis Kronenberger (London, 1977), p. 156.

CHAPTER 4

[1] See *The Letters of Mrs Gaskell*, p. 33.

[2] For detailed discussion of nineteenth-century Unitarianism see Earl Morse Wilbur, *A History of Unitarianism in Translyvania, England, and America* (Cambridge, Mass., 1952) and W. Arthur Boggs, 'Reflections of Unitarianism in Mrs. Gaskell's Novels' (unpublished doctoral dissertation, University of California, 1950). Examples of the Unitarian principles listed: William E. Channing, *Works*, third edition, 6 vols (Glasgow, 1840–4), III, 83–4, 88; James Martineau, John Hamilton Thom and Henry Giles, *Unitarianism Defended* (Liverpool, 1839), Lecture XII, 50.

[3] Channing, III, 60.

[4] Edgar Wright, *Mrs. Gaskell: The Basis for Reassessment* (London, 1965), p. 43.

[5] Thomas Paine, *The Rights of Man*, Everyman's Library, 718 (1915; reprinted, London, 1966), p. 44.

[6] Arthur Pollard, *Mrs Gaskell: Novelist and Biographer* (Manchester, 1965), p. 51.

[7] See my article on 'The Writer as Reader in *Mary Barton*', *The Durham University Journal*, new series, 36 (1974), 92–102.

[8] John Forster, *The Life of Charles Dickens*, edited by A. J. Hoppé, 2 vols (London, 1966), I, 282–3.

[9] For an analysis of Elizabeth Gaskell's use of a parable in her portrayal of character and landscape in *Ruth* (1853), see my article on 'The Sinner as Heroine: A Study of Mrs Gaskell's *Ruth* and the Bible', *The Durham University Journal*, new series, 37 (1976), 148–61.

[10] Raymond Williams, *Culture and Society 1780–1950* (London, 1958; reprinted, Harmondsworth, 1961), p. 101.

[11] *Mary Barton: A Tale of Manchester Life*, edited by Stephen Gill, Penguin English Library (Harmondsworth, 1970), p. 21.

[12] Louis Cazamian wrote on some of these texts in his pioneering study of social-problem fiction:

The mill-owners were fortified by their personal relations with God and their severe, narrow-minded morality. And they based their sturdy respect for the rights of property on the Ten Commandments. . . .

But Evangelicalism and Bible Christianity carried within themselves the seeds of a revolt against individualistic morality. The teaching of the Bible might be used to sanction enlightened self-interest, but it also forbade its excessive or cruel pursuit. Evangelicalism took as its daily bread precepts like 'Do unto others as you would that they should do to you;' 'Thou canst not serve God and Mammon;' the parable of Dives and Lazarus, and the oriental horror of the golden calf: all served to inhibit greed, and put a check to the advance of industrial self-interest.

The Social Novel in England 1830–1850: Dickens, Disraeli, Mrs Gaskell, Kingsley (1903), translated by Martin Fido (London, 1973), pp. 211–12.

CHAPTER 5

[1] Alexander Welsh discusses Dickens's apocalyptic references to time in other novels in his *The City in Dickens* (Oxford, 1971), e.g., pp. 226–8.

[2] Wolfgang Iser examines the changing nature of the 'implied' reader in fiction since the *Pilgrim's Progress* in *The Implied Reader* (Baltimore, 1974).

[3] See George Bornstein, 'Miscultivated Field and Corrupted Garden: Imagery in *Hard Times*', *Nineteenth-Century Fiction,* 26 (1971–2), 158–70. In the last section of his article, Bornstein mentions some of the allusions which I examine, but concentrates mainly on cultivation and related biblical texts.

[4] Geoffrey Rowell, *Hell and the Victorians: A Study of the Nineteenth-Century Theological Controversies Concerning Eternal Punishment and the Future Life* (Oxford, 1974), p. 31.

[5] See William Oddie, *Dickens and Carlyle: The Question of Influence* (London, 1972), and Michael Goldberg, *Carlyle and Dickens* (Athens, Georgia, 1972).

[6] Goldberg, p. 81.

[7] Bornstein, p. 161.

[8] Francis D. Klingender, *Art and the Industrial Revolution* (1947), edited and revised by Arthur Elton (London, 1972), ills 58, 59.

[9] Theophilus Lindsey, *Sermons, with Appropriate Prayers Annexed,* 2 vols (London, 1810), II, 333.

CHAPTER 6

[1] Discussion of Edward Casaubon's sources has tended to centre on contemporary life sources, Victorian scholars on whom George Eliot may or may not have modelled her character. (For example, see Richard Ellmann, 'Dorothea's husbands: some biographical speculations', *Times Literary Supplement*, 16 February 1973, pp. 165–8, and subsequent correspondence.) Casaubon's name has led source-hunters to Isaac Casaubon's biographer, Mark Pattison, who met George Eliot shortly before she began *Middlemarch* and through whom she could have learnt details of Isaac's private life and scholarly habits of work. George Eliot and her contemporaries could have gleaned some of their impressions of Isaac Casaubon from Pattison's anonymous review article on

Ephemerides Isaaci Casauboni and Nisard's *Le Triumvirat Littéraire au XVI. Siècle; Juste Lipse, Joseph Scaliger, Isaac Casaubon* in the *Quarterly Review*, 93 (1853), 462–500. Certain passages would certainly have fired the imagination of the creator of Edward Casaubon: 'Matrimony did not detain him long from his books' (p. 471); 'He was not . . . free from the weakness with which we are so familiar in the commentators of Shakspeare, of piling up quotation upon quotation for the sole purpose of displaying his reading' (p. 481, note); 'If we go with Casaubon into his study we find him beset with difficulties, and groaning with weariness' (p. 500). Pattison's most extensive work of scholarship, the biography of Casaubon, was published a few years after *Middlemarch*, in 1875. The section in which Pattison describes Casaubon's 'Characteristics' includes passages which are highly suggestive when juxtaposed with George Eliot's description of her belated scholar:

> Casaubon must be reckoned among those who hoarded more than they could ever use.
> Whatever comes up, he can pour out an inexhaustible stock of suggested parallels. . . . He thought of the object through the words of the ancients.
> He deceived himself into thinking that he had made progress in writing, when the material was heaped up only in his memory.
> Casaubon's books are now consigned to one common oblivion.

Mark Pattison, *Isaac Casaubon 1559–1614,* second edition, edited by Henry Nettleship (Oxford, 1892), pp. 423–4, 427, 433.

[2] In the manuscript and first edition there are no inverted commas around 'affable archangel' (see British Museum Add. MS 34,035, f.79). George Eliot made her allusion a marked quotation when she corrected the proofs of the second edition (1874). David Carroll has pointed out to me that she tended to mark or attribute her quotations more clearly as she revised. Thus, for example, she explicitly attributed a marked quotation ('passionate prodigality') only when correcting the proofs of the second edition, inserting 'to use Sir Thomas Browne's phrase' (37). This suggests that she wanted as many of her readers as possible to notice her allusions and recognise their adopted texts.

[3] The contrast between Bulstrode and Caleb Garth is interesting in this respect. Bulstrode used to preach in his youth and the texts are 'there still' (53). The vestiges of the 'letter' of these texts and of the worn phrases of the Evangelical preacher can be identified in the language of his private thoughts after the arrival of Raffles, but the 'spirit' is long dead. Caleb, on the other hand, is 'haunted by a sense of Biblical phraseology' whenever he has a 'feeling of awe', though he can hardly give a 'strict quotation' (40). In his conduct, as in his speech, he is living proof that 'the letter killeth, but the spirit giveth life'.

[4] The manuscript ends more positively: 'owing to many of those who sleep in unvisited tombs, having lived a hidden life nobly.'

[5] *Westminster Review*, 134 (1890). See *George Eliot, 'Middlemarch': A Casebook*, edited by Patrick Swinden (London, 1972), p. 21.

[6] *Athenaeum*, 7 December 1872. See *Casebook*, p. 39.

[7] *Spectator*, 1 June 1872. See *Casebook*, p. 34.

[8] See *Quarry for Middlemarch*, edited by Anna Theresa Kitchel, Supplement to *Nineteenth-Century Fiction*, 4 (1950), and John Clark Pratt, 'A *Middlemarch* Miscellany: An Edition, with Introduction and Notes, of George

Eliot's 1868–1871 Notebook' (unpublished doctoral dissertation, University of Princeton, 1965).

CHAPTER 7

[1] See J. A. Sutherland, *Victorian Novelists and Publishers* (London, 1976), p. 188.
[2] *The Letters of George Meredith*, edited by C. L. Cline, 3 vols (Oxford, 1970), I, 130.
[3] Marie Corelli's anecdote to this effect is quoted by Lionel Stevenson in *The Ordeal of George Meredith: A Biography* (New York, 1953), p. 302.
[4] *Meredith: The Critical Heritage*, edited by Ioan Williams, Critical Heritage Series, general editor B. C. Southam (London, 1971), p. 202.
[5] *Meredith: The Critical Heritage*, p. 222.
[6] The similarity between Mrs Mountstuart Jenkinson and Mrs Cadwallader has struck other readers, including the anonymous reviewer in the *Saturday Review* of 1879 who called Meredith's character 'a kind of good-natured Mrs Cadwallader'. See *Meredith: The Critical Heritage*, p. 221.
[7] Interestingly, Dickens plays upon the word *circle* in his Carlylean warning to the people who assemble at Chesney Wold for a house-party:

There is perhaps more Dandyism at Chesney Wold than the brilliant and distinguished circle will find good for itself in the long run. For it is, even with the stillest and politest circles, as with the circle the necromancer draws around him–very strange appearances may be seen in active motion outside. With this difference; that, being realities and not phantoms, there is the greater danger of their breaking in. (12)

[8] Gillian Beer finds a number of similar resonances. Having discussed Robert Mayo's article on the Willow Pattern analogue in *The Egoist* (see note 10 below), she suggests that Austin Dobson's *Proverbs in Porcelain* (1877) 'may be another pointer to Willoughby's unease', and that, in the breaking of the vase, Meredith 'may be invoking echoes from Restoration and Augustan comedy: the famous double-entendre scene of "viewing the china" in Wycherley's *The Country Wife*, Pope's image in *The Rape of the Lock*'. See *Meredith: A Change of Masks–A Study of the Novels* (London, 1970), pp. 131–2.
[9] For a discussion of synecdoche see Daniel Smirlock, 'Rough Truth: Synecdoche and Interpretation in *The Egoist*', *Nineteenth-Century Fiction*, 31(1976–7), 313–28.
[10] Robert D. Mayo, '*The Egoist* and the Willow Pattern', *ELH*, 9 (1942), 71–8 (pp. 72–3).
[11] Daniel R. Schwarz, 'The Porcelain-Pattern Leitmotif in Meredith's *The Egoist*', *The Victorian Newsletter*, no. 33 (Spring 1968), 26–8 (pp. 26, 28).
[12] In having Clara awaken Vernon Whitford under the lovely but sterile tree, 'Meredith suggests that she must awaken his manhood so that he may escape the graceful sterility of life at Patterne', according to Michael Sundell in 'The Functions of Flitch in *The Egoist*', *Nineteenth-Century Fiction*, 24 (1969–70), 227–35 (p. 230).
[13] Review of *The Egoist* in *Blackwood's* (1880). See *Meredith: The Critical Heritage*, p. 236.

CHAPTER 8

[1] *Thomas Hardy: The Critical Heritage*, edited by R. G. Cox, Critical Heritage Series, general editor B. C. Southam (London and New York, 1970), p. xxxvi.

[2] *Thomas Hardy and his Readers: A Selection of Contemporary Reviews*, edited by Laurence Lerner and John Holmstrom (London, 1968), p. 80.

[3] See Chapter 6, note 1.

[4] See Enid Huws Jones, *Mrs Humphry Ward* (London, 1973), pp. 82–3.

[5] The Gladstone Papers, vol. 418, British Museum Add. MS 44,503, ff.184–5.

[6] Stephen Gwynn, *Mrs Humphry Ward*, Writers of the Day Series, edited by Bertram Christian (London, 1917), p. 30.

[7] See Janet Penrose Trevelyan, *The Life of Mrs Humphry Ward* (London, 1923), p. 75.

[8] W. E. Gladstone, '"Robert Elsmere" and the Battle of Belief', *Nineteenth Century*, 23 (1888), 766–88 (p. 769).

[9] William S. Peterson has also recognised the parallel between the Thornburghs and the Bennets. See his *Victorian Heretic: Mrs Humphry Ward's 'Robert Elsmere'* (Leicester, 1976), p. 142.

[10] Elsmere misquotes 'She was a Phantom of delight', 12: 'A Spirit, yet a Woman too!' Judging by the high number of (often slight) misquotations in *Robert Elsmere*, I think it likely that Mary Ward did not bother to check her adopted texts, particularly when quoting works which were fairly familiar to her, such as Wordsworth's poems. Hereafter I direct attention to misquotations by giving the reference to the original location, prefaced by 'cf.', in my text.

[11] Biographical confirmation also came to light when Peterson published a newly discovered letter from Mary Ward in which she acknowledged that 'some of the *colouring* of the country parish part' was suggested by the *Life* of Kingsley, a 'favourite book' of hers. See Peterson, *Victorian Heretic*, pp. 134–5.

[12] Mary Ward, 'Some Thoughts on Charlotte Brontë', foreword to *Charlotte Brontë 1816–1916: A Centenary Memorial*, edited by Butler Wood for the Brontë Society (London, 1917), p. 27.

[13] Anonymous review of 'Novels', *Saturday Review*, 65 (1888), 356.

CHAPTER 9

[1] Hardy busily collected literary fragments and quotations (his 'Literary Notes') in the year preceding the writing of the *Return*, clearly preparing himself for a major literary work. See Robert Gittings, *The Older Hardy* (London, 1978), pp. 2–6, and *The Literary Notes of Thomas Hardy*, edited by Lennart A. Björk, Gothenburg Studies in English, 29, 2 vols (Gothenburg, 1974), I, xviii–xix, xxxv.

[2] Louis Crompton, 'The Sunburnt God: Ritual and Tragic Myth in *The Return of the Native*', *Boston University Studies in English*, 4 (1960), 229–40 (p. 232).

[3] For example, in the 'Midnight Baptism' sequence, omitted from the *Graphic*

and published separately in the *Fortnightly Review* (1 May 1891), part of Hardy's description of Tess preparing to christen her child by candlelight reads as follows in the first edition of the novel: 'her high enthusiasm having a transfiguring effect upon the face which had been her undoing, showing it as a thing of immaculate beauty, with a touch of dignity which was almost regal' (14). Material which followed this passage in the manuscript was not inserted in the first and subsequent editions: '. . . that seemed regal, exhibiting Cleopatra's majesty & Atalanta's better part interfused' (*Tess of the d'Urbervilles*, British Museum Add. MS 38, 182, ff.99–100). The omission of these allusions in the first edition is an improvement, for without them the specifically Christian connotations of Tess's momentary 'transfiguring' are not blurred by other associations.

4 *The Return of the Native*, University College, Dublin MS 11, f. 72a.

5 *Belgravia*, 34 (January–February 1878), 502.

6 See John Paterson, '*The Return of the Native* as Antichristian Document', *Nineteenth-Century Fiction*, 14 (1959–60), 111–27; David J. de Laura, '"The Ache of Modernism" in Hardy's Later Novels', *ELH*, 34 (1967), 380–99.

7 See S. F. Johnson, 'Hardy and Burke's "Sublime"', in *Style in Prose Fiction: English Institute Essays 1958*, edited by Harold C. Martin (New York and London, 1959), pp. 55–86.

8 Jeremy V. Steele has suggested that Hardy probably had a different Ovidian episode (*Fasti*, I.391–440) 'in mind when he wrote up the Chaseborough dance' ('Which Ovid in the Hay-Shed? A Note on "Tess of the d'Urbervilles"', *Notes and Queries*, new series, 24 (1977), 430–2 (p. 431)). Although Steele shows that the *Fasti* passage may well have been an important *source*, the word 'metamorphosed' in *Tess* cannot be brushed aside as 'an unexceptional element in [Hardy's] latinate vocabulary' (Steele, p. 431). The classical *allusions*, juxtaposed with the word 'metamorphosed', read as references to Ovid's more famous work.

9 See, for example, *Charles Darwin: His Life*, edited by Francis Darwin (London, 1902), p. 167 (Lamarck); *The Life and Letters of Charles Darwin*, edited by Francis Darwin, 3 vols (London, 1887), I, 82 (Darwin); Herbert Spencer, *Essays: Scientific, Political, and Speculative*, 2 vols (London and Edinburgh, 1883), I, 381 (Spencer).

10 See Lionel Stevenson, *Darwin Among the Poets* (1932; reprinted, New York, 1963), pp. 243–4, 277.

11 J. T. Laird, *The Shaping of 'Tess of the d'Urbervilles'* (Oxford, 1975), p. 58. Laird's comments on the Chaseborough allusions end with a more general statement:

Hardy's debt to Ovid, and especially to the *Metamorphoses*, would seem to be somewhat more wide-ranging and deeper in *Tess* than has hitherto been recognized. For not only does Ovid seem to have provided the specific allusions: he also may well have been one of the main models for Hardy's employment of pastoral landscape as symbol and for some of the individual themes, as well as for aspects of characterization. (Laird, p. 57)

He does not follow up these interesting comments, but quotes Charles Paul Segal on landscape in the *Metamorphoses*: 'Ovid achieves a special and characteristic effect . . . by using peaceful sylvan scenes as the setting for violence, often sexual violence' (Laird, p. 57).

CHAPTER 10

[1] *The Letters of Henry James*, selected and edited by Percy Lubbock, 2 vols (London, 1920), I, 306.

[2] Douglas's and the governess's accounts of her meeting with her master in London and her arrival at Bly are both vaguely reminiscent of Jane Eyre's story. The young, inexperienced governess is strongly attracted to her master, a 'bachelor in the prime of life'. Mrs Grose, like Mrs Fairfax at Thornfield, presides over the country house in the master's absence, and seems to withhold some secret from the governess. Flora is not unlike Adèle in certain respects, flitting about the house like a 'sprite' (1). Although rather labyrinthine in style, parts of the opening paragraph of the governess's narrative could almost have been written by Jane Eyre (1). The governess's account of hearing a distant cry on her first night at the house (1), and her overt reference to 'a mystery of Udolpho or an insane, an unmentionable relative kept in unsuspected confinement' (4), prompt one to ask how we are to respond to the Gothic machinery of the tale. There is, of course, no simple answer. Allusion seems to be part of an elaborate, teasing game, in which questions raised in the reader's mind are never answered 'in any literal, vulgar way'.

[3] It is worth recalling here that F. R. Leavis called that 'astonishing work', *Wuthering Heights*, 'a kind of sport' in *The Great Tradition* (1948; reprinted, Harmondsworth, 1962), p. 38. This comment helps to explain the rise of the novel's critical stock during our own century, particularly among critics whose interests are different from Leavis's.

[4] *Literary Essays of Ezra Pound*, edited by T. S. Eliot (London, 1954), p. 405.

[5] Avrom Fleishman writes: 'Virginia Woolf is to be seen as an artist fully at one with the modern movement of experimentation and innovation, but, as is the case with the other major figures of the period, her novelty is most often a variation on traditional themes.' He also comments that, in *Mrs Dalloway*, Woolf 'defines character, adumbrates themes, and introduces a pattern of dual impulse – toward life, toward death – based on her use of literary quotations and other elements of her cultural tradition'. 'Virginia Woolf: Tradition and Modernity', in *Forms of Modern British Fiction*, edited by Alan Warren Friedman (Austin and London, 1975), pp. 133–63 (pp. 161, 151).

[6] See Fleishman's comments in colloquium in *Forms of Modern British Fiction*, p. 213.

[7] Peter K. Garrett, 'Double Plots and Dialogical Form in Victorian Fiction', *Nineteenth-Century Fiction*, 32 (1977–8), 1–17 (p. 2).

[8] Jonathan Culler, *Structuralist Poetics: Structuralism, Linguistics and the Study of Literature* (London, 1975), p. 30.

[9] See Chapter 6, note 2.

Index